Dedication to

I dedicate this book to my birthplace, my haven - West Bengal. It has given me so much that can never be repayed but through 'Bengal 21' it's my humble attempt to add a small bit to the mesmerising culture and unmatched literature of my state.

Shagufta Hanaphie

First Published in December 2021

ISBN: 978-93-5472-963-8

BLUEROSE PUBLISHERS

www.bluerosepublishers.com

info@bluerosepublishers.com

+91 8882 898 898

Cover Design:

Ananda Ghosh

Typographic Design:

Namrata Saini

Distributed by: BlueRose, Amazon, Flipkart, Shopclues

Preface

"Nothing can dim the light that shines from within"

Bengal 21 chronicles the lives of some inspirational personalities who have helped shape the contours of people close to them send in some way, the whole of India. The compilation includes some outstanding women, entrepreneurs, artists, philanthropists, social reformers, game changers and many others.

Every common man or woman with his/her sheer grit and hard work achieves success and should be given a chance to share his/her story with the rest, for they may find inspiration and strength to go on. **'Bengal 21'** is full of insights, personal moments and life experiences that give us an understanding of their journey of success. By going through the life journeys of these 21 people, I'm sure we'll be successful in evoking the reader to identify their inner fire and potential, because I strongly believe that each one of us is born with the strength and ability to make a tangible change in the world. How these people inspired themselves to achieve dreams and how they went about accomplishing so much, is what **Bengal 21** captures so marvellously.

I'm sure you'll enjoy reading the lives of these 21 Personalities who have influenced us and are a source of constant inspiration and motivation for all of us.

Each story includes life sketch, quotes, poems, successes, failures and awards associated with him/her to inspire the readers and satisfy their curious instincts.

I'm truly honoured to learn about the lives of these inspiring people and I do hope that once you open the pages of the book to read their success stories, you will discover for yourself how fast you can imbibe their traits to make it big in your life.

Happy reading!!;

Author Profile

"Either write something worth reading or do something worth writing"

Everything you do or say is public relations. Perceptions are formed by the words we say or what we do. How we communicate is an art and SHE (Shagufta Hanaphie Events) has been working on PR – the key component of communication for many years. SHE has always believed in bringing out and nurturing unheard stories

and events which need recognition and applause. Working on the same lines of magnetizing and retaining exceptionally talented individuals who have worked tremendously well in their own fields and are a major source of inspiration, SHE has compiled Bengal 21 – a book based on the lives of 21 individuals from Bengal. Their stories have the ability to make you cry, laugh, feel angry but in totality they have the power to motivate and inspire you to become better versions of yourself.

Founder of SHE, Shagufta Hanaphie, with 17 years of remarkable and extremely successful experience in PR and communication, is a true example of someone who has the courage to fight every battle life has in store for her, but she still lives each day with unmatched vigour and determination, only to emerge as a winner every time. With a vision to help individuals and businesses showcase their talent in order to build their brand, she decided to publish a book on the lives of 21 people of Bengal whose stories need to be heard and taken inspiration from. These stories have been written so that others can see fragments of themselves. Stories are one of the most powerful ways to guide, teach and inspire people. Inspirational stories move past creating a sense of connection and allow the reader to identify with the stories. The best and most beautiful things in the world cannot be seen or even touched. They must be felt with the heart and these 21 stories from Bengal will make you understand that emotion in the best possible way.

Contents

Conveying Emotions Through Art

Wasim Kapoor

Some painters transform the sun into a yellow spot, others spot a yellow spot in the sun

Being an artist isn't just about putting pencil to paper, or brush to canvas, art means so much more than that, to so many people. Art is a way of seeing the world, a way of expression and sometimes just a feeling to simply create something. Art may be a way to explore your world or your imagination. Art may inspire a beginning painter to take steps into learning a new medium or an accomplished artist to experiment with a new technique. Art is teaching, art is learning, art is exciting, empowering and a true expression of love.

Among the many artists who have walked down history and those who belong to the present generation, **Wasim Kapoor** is someone who can be called 'Art Personified'. Having been confined to a hospital for the formative 12 years of his life because of a fall at the age of six months, Wasim had no idea back then that he would lead a life of an artist and would not only be known at the national level but would also create a magnificent niche for himself globally.

From the hospital bed, he would try and copy the pictures of fruits and animals from his brother's school books when the latter would come to see him. Seeing the keen interest of art in young Wasim, his father appointed a drawing teacher for him who would come to the hospital and teach him the nuances of art. The regular rendezvous with the art teacher introduced Wasim to a whole new world of colours and figures. As time flew by and Wasim grew up, his father enrolled him into Indian art college, Kolkata. Even though the principal and teachers of the college did not understand how someone like Wasim could sit and learn drawing for so many hours because of his physical condition, both Wasim and his father were adamant and wanted the best teachers to teach him. Their decision was absolutely perfect as it did not take much time for Wasim to create an impression on his teachers.

When he was in first year of Art College, he would quickly learn his classes and then go on to the second and third year classes to learn from the students there too. During his career span, Wasim was conferred upon with innumerable honors and awards. He feels himself to be extremely lucky to have found the opportunity to study under the tutelage of many renowned artists and noted personalities from that era.

Wasim Kapoor shared a beautiful relationship with his father, an eminent poet Salik Luckhnawi who was the proud recipient of the Padma Shri Award. Due to him being a popular figure, Wasim grew up in the company of many renowned poets, film stars, music directors and politicians. He would often sit with them while they would have debates and discussions on various worldly topics. This exposure helped him garner keen interest in literature, art and intricacies of human nature.

As he continued to create masterpieces with this brush, Wasim depicted various agonies and painful emotions of mankind. He was fortunate to get his first big break because of his father when his friend asked young Wasim to create something for the Iran society's centenary celebrations.

Wasim is an artist who believes in surrealism which is a bridge between the dream world and reality. Recipient of innumerable awards and accolades, both nationally and internationally, Wasim is happy to lead a simple life where he does not believe in competition, judgement, jealousy or hatred. His simplistic nature is vastly depicted in his paintings and demeanour as well. Success for him is a continuous cycle which includes the love of his family, friends and surroundings and does not believe in crediting himself alone for his success. He firmly believes in preaching the aspect that good things come to good people and one should never stop doing their best if they wish to achieve success.

Wasim Kapoor's paintings are known to depict human agony and pain and this is quite obvious when one looks at his artwork as he is famous for using the most basic colours black and white for the masterpieces that he creates. He feels it is necessary to speak for those who cannot speak for themselves. This was the reason why he came up with the boy and girl child series, the Burkha series, the prostitute series, the rickshaw series and the Christ series. He feels every artist should take up the responsibility of highlighting the unjust issues, crisis and problems of the society so that solutions can be thought of and the world could become a better place for one and all.

Wasim's paintings have been appreciated and loved all across the globe by eminent personalities and also adorn various magnificent institutions such as Parliament House, Rajya Sabha, Victoria Memorial along with renowned museums like National Gallery of Medium Art Delhi, Birla Academy of Art &

Culture Kolkata, Lalit Kala Academy New Delhi and many more.

Not only in India but around the world too, Wasim has a magnificent fan following of art connoisseurs who love his depiction of human emotions and struggles. For years, he has derived his ideas from social reality and from the omnipresent sufferings of mankind. All his subjects, whether Jesus Christ, the hard working rickshaw puller, the destitute prostitutes or the exploited children, reflect pain and angst which they have been suffering from decades at the hands of the cruel society. Wasim Kapoor is very well-known for his black attire that he adorns regularly. When he shifted to the colour is unknown to him but he says that since the time his paintings started portraying only black and white, his attire changed too. The images that he paints are a reflection of what he feels.

Wasim Kapoor from a very young age managed to carve a niche for himself at a time when there were various veteran artists ruling the industry. But due to his simplicity, the subjects he decided to paint and the message his paintings conveyed, he successfully managed to rise and shine.

As a message to the young and budding artists, Wasim wants to convey that pursuing art is a great idea only if one is not looking at a shorter way to achieve success. Art or painting is a slow process which involves a fair amount of recognition, criticism, perseverance and courage. If your painting is extraordinary, you do not need to care about what the world has to say. It will achieve success if it is truly marvellous. Never stop doing your job and follow your passion. A very strong message that Wasim

Kapoor wishes to convey to the younger generation of artists is to stay unique and not to copy the styles of other artists. Try to make a mark of your own.

Wasim Kapoor believes that the best day of his life was when he fell off the bed at six months of age because it made him come face to face with the purpose of his life. Mankind has been creating art and appreciating its beauty since its beginning and becoming an artist can be quite a daunting prospect but whether you are interested in acrylic paint, oil painting or more water colour etc, it's never too late to follow your passion and become an artist. Painting must be fertile. It must give birth to a world, it must fertilise your imagination.

You're an artist, not Picasso or Vangogh
You're an artist, not professional I know
You're the creator of your own world
You're the designer of your life

Mold the clay around your mood
Paint the picture that you choose
Do the things you want to do
Be the artiest, just be you

Create the vision in your mind
Mix the colors that life combines
Be your best friend, just be you
That's Picasso and Vangogh

A Journey of Success and Motivation

Prof. Dr. Sujoy Biswas

"Successful people don't do different things, they do things differently"

But what is that difference. The difference is they put in the hard work even when it hurts.

What we all need is some motive in life in order to reach our destination. Becoming a motivational speaker or deciding to become one, calls for dedication. Dedication to share what you know and to inspire others. All this happens with a fair amount of commitment. Every speaker has someone in their life who acts as their inspiration. Whether it is the people who influence or their own inner passion that pushes them forward. Your motivation could be as simple as helping other people rise up. To achieve your purpose in life, you need to particularly develop three values - hard work, patience and determination.

Prof. Dr. Sujoy Biswas is a true example of a concoction of the above mentioned values and because of his power of these set of values and due to his consistent work towards interacting with people and excelling in his public speaking skills, he developed a tremendously positive attitude. And, this mixed with this keen interest in philosophy, helped him in becoming a great motivator.

Born and brought up in Kolkata, **Prof. Dr. Sujoy Biswas** is currently the Director and CEO of Techno India University and Techno India Group. After completing his schooling from South point high school, Dr. Biswas completed his B tech in Civil engineering from Jadavpur University before going on to do an

M Tech in the same field as well. Dr. Biswas secured a first class first position in his MBA examination and received a gold medal too.

Dr. Biswas started his illustrious and inspiring career with M.N Dastur and company, the largest steel plant consultancy in the world. After serving this organisation for 12 long years, he joined DSQ software limited for a couple of years. As a part of his amazing career, he also headed West Bengal Police Computerization and Kolkata police computerization for the next seven years. He is currently serving the very prestigious Techno India group for the last 12 ½ years. He is also the mentor for Civil Engineering Architecture and Management department of all institutions under the huge umbrella of the Techno India Group.

Prof. Dr. Sujoy Biswas is an outstanding and much sought after speaker who believes that speaking skills are something that should be kept sharpened similar to that of an edge of a knife because the more you do it, the more you get skilled. Dr. Biswas has never stopped doing it and believes that consistency not only in public speaking but any in any field definitely leads to excellence. He strongly believes that a little perseverance is what it takes to make things happen. Keep on doing stuff that you think you could be good at, keep improvising your skills and you surely can make it big.

Prof. Dr. Biswas is also the anchor and director of one of the most popular and unique celebrity show "Joyer Pathey Sange Sujoy" which has been successfully running since the past four and a half years and is currently in its 275th week. To spread the message of staying safe during these unprecedented times, Dr.

Biswas also runs a programme named "Korona Kahini Sange Sujoy" which completed 80 episodes in High News Channel. Due to his immense talent and proficiency in music, Dr. Biswas is also the lead singer of the musical band "TROYEE". Among the various attributes to his shining persona, Prof. Dr. Biswas is an avid social worker and the patron of the Lions Club, Rotary Club , "Dakshin Kolkata Manashi"and NGO "Srijon Sabha" which supports children with autism a NGO which supports the less privileged section of the society.

Prof. Dr. Sujoy Biswas realised he had the spark of being a motivational speaker when he started addressing the Techno India students during class hours and academic program gatherings. While focusing on the content that he delivered during his speeches, he also paid lots of attention his body language and style of delivery and he has excelled in motivating others under all conditions.

Dr. Biswas believes that the flame of aspirations must be so ardent that no obstacle would be able to dissolve it. He loves to motivate people around him and according to him, life is full of struggles and one must know that strength and growth comes only through continuous effort and hard work. All our struggles are a form of a training process that prepare us for the next step. He wants to believe in the fact that no one can motivate one another, in fact they can only be inspired to achieve their goals.

Dr. Biswas loves to interact with the younger generation and enjoys working with them so that he can help them shape their future. Another important aspect, he believes in is that knowledge cannot be taken away or snatched from someone. Every human being has a unique story to tell which actually ends up becoming a life lesson for someone else. His mission is to enable students to get in touch with their inner strengths and use them as building blocks for a successful future.

Prof. Dr. Sujoy Biswas believes that education is the most powerful weapon which can be used to change the world and he strives to do just that by talking to the youngsters. He seeks to foster increased engagement with students and adults to not only help youth achieve their highest potential but also to raise their happiness and fulfillment index. He feels happy thinking that his motivational speeches might successfully create a minor shift in their outlook today which will surely have a huge impact in the years to come.

Full of humility and respect for others, Dr. Biswas is that kind if a person who is difficult to come across these days. With so many different accolades attached to his name, he still manages to remain the humble, respectful and lovable person that he always strives to be. Sometimes, it's hard to remember that we need to be humble to get along in the world. Our sense of pride can get in our way and cause us to make mistakes. The things we brag about may even be false. Often people build up their humility so much, it's a form of bragging in itself. But, Dr. Biswas even after interacting with a long list of renowned doctors, industrialists, celebrity's from the world of performing arts and many more, has his head set firmly on his strong shoulders and believes to practice all that he preaches to others. His popularity among children, young adults, adults and elderly is proof of his immense fan following.

Prof. Dr. Sujoy Biswas feels himself lucky to have been married to a highly educated and qualified woman Prof Dr Chandrani Biswas. Prof Dr Chandrani Biswas is an alumnus of St.Xaviers College, Kolkata Jawaharlal Nehru University and Jadavpur University. She completed her Graduation with English Honours (BA – Hons) from St Xaviers College and was a top rank holder in Calcutta University. She also was a rank holder in her Masters in English (MA) from Jawaharlal Nehru University and her theisis in her M.Phil course was considered one of the best in her time and came out as a book named " Woman and War" published from Books Plus Publishers, New Delhi. Later on she completed her PhD from Jadavpur University. Currently she is an Associate Professor, Department of English, St.Xavier's College (Autonomous) Kolkata. Prof Dr Chandrani Biswas not only understands her husband Prof Dr Sujoy Biswas's passion and profession but is also standing like a rock behind him.

He attributes his success to not only his wife but also to his god gifted daughter Vaishna Biswas who is a source of inspiration for him too. Vaishna ranked in her secondary and higher secondary examination and also a top ranker in her B Tech (Electronics and Communication Engineering) from Jadavpur University and is currently working with TRAI (Telecom Regulatory Authority of India).

Dr. Biswas is a world class, dynamic and captivating speaker. It is said that an inspirational speaker is easy to find but a motivational speaker that can connect with the heart and soul of the audience and deliver a message with substance and a unique style is very rare. Words have incredible power. They can make people's hearts soar, or they can make people's hearts sore.

When we share with someone else,
Something valuable to us
You may find out later on,
To them they feel they were blessed.

Some of us have lots to give,
And some of us do not.
If someone could benefit,
Why not give them a shot.

Sharing is a wonderful thing,
Especially to those you've shared with.
There are a lot of kind people out there,
And that is not a myth.

So next time you see someone,
Who could benefit from something you can share.
Don't hold back and look away,
Be kind and answer their prayer.

A benevolent woman with a heart of gold!!

Seema Bahri

"You know someone is truly special when the most beautiful thing they have on is a kind soul"

Over the course of your life, you meet all kinds of people. Some are compassionate, honest, good and loving. While there are others who are selfish, jealous and manipulative. But there are some kind of people who are unique as they are blessed with a heart of gold.

Seema Bahri is unequivocally a woman who's heart is big enough to contain all the kindness and love in the world. Seema is the much loved and respected headmistress of The Basic Funda School in Kolkata, India. Born in Patna, Bihar into a business class Punjabi family, she was the fourth child and the youngest amongst her siblings. Being the youngest member of a close knit joint family, she had various emotional branches to help her in her all round development. Seema's maternal grandfather was a professor and her mother Mrs. Prabha Arora completed her Masters in Sanskrit. Thus even though she belonged to a business family, a lot of importance was given to education and her father Mr. B.M Arora, who is a self-made man always emphasized on hard work. Seeing him shower love and affection on all children whether they were his own, or his relatives or belonged to his employees, Seema grew up with similar set of values. She did her schooling from Notre Dame Academy Patna and completed her graduation with honours in Economics from Patna Women's College. Post marriage, she was extremely lucky to have found a very supportive partner in her husband Sameer Bahri and children Astha and

Devyansh, who stood with her in all her endeavours and encouraged her to complete a diploma in interior designing. She was although trained to be a designer, she began her entrepreneurial journey by designing and selling jewellery.

Even though she had never received formal education, required to take care of children with special needs, her passion to do the same helped her to realize her dream. We all experience turning points in life. The decisions we make can take us from one path to another, sometimes in an instant. Seema had never thought that her turning point was yet to arrive and that her interview in Kangaroo Kids, Delhi would change her life forever and take her to a path which was not only amazing and beautiful but also very fulfilling and satisfying. After having taken care of a few special children during her tenure in Kangaroo Kids, she shifted to Kolkata and once her kids were settled, she decided to open an inclusive school in the year 2013 – The Basic Funda School with the motto – If they don't learn the way you teach, maybe you should teach the way they learn.

The idea to open an inclusive school came to Seema when she was teaching in Delhi and also when she had shifted to Kolkata and would escort her kids to school. She decided to place students with special needs in the same environment as other students their age, who did not have special needs. She strongly believes that all children belong to the same classroom environment, no matter what. She practices and spreads the message that children with special needs, thrive better in standard classrooms for a variety of reasons. Seema also feels that children who are placed in standard classrooms generally have a higher self esteem than those who are isolated in separate classrooms. She aspires to open a chain of inclusive schools, so as to spread the message of inclusivity far and wide. She strongly believes that inclusive education is a dynamic ever evolving approach that requires ongoing reflection and continuous enhancement.

Seema is extremely grateful to her team who are all professionally trained and are valuable assets for the school. We can easily come across her gorgeous soul when she gets teary eyed while talking about her students. One child among many others who has left a deep mark on her heart was one of the first students in her school. Seema once narrated to me the fond remembrance she has of that day. This little girl had walked into the school premises holding her mothers hand and just like any other 2 ½ year old, she too was extremely shy and was continuously clinging on to her mother but the moment she saw Seema, she left her mom's hand and ran to hug Seema. This was and still is the magic that the Headmistress of The Basic Funda School, Ms. Seema Bahri has on her students. She also remembers the time when the lease of the school building had got over and she was searching for a place to shift. All the parents of the students studying there got together and helped her acquire a place as soon as possible. Seema feels immensely lucky to have found unconditional love and support from not only her family and friends but also from her students and their parents.

Seema is forever inspiring people around her with her belief in equality and oneness and this is the reason she had decided to open an inclusive school where all kinds of children, whether normal or special could get a chance to study, interact and play together.

Her philanthropic deeds during the times of Amphan and the pandemic have helped innumerable people, as she is always ready to help all those who need support. According to her, philanthropy has always come naturally to her and she is also grateful to her friends who have kept her involved in their areas of social work. She has also volunteered at an inclusive school Alokdhara for 2 ½ years and is associated with a few very famous NGO's since last decade.

She has always succeeded in spreading a strong positive aura among the people who she has come in contact with and she is a strong believer of karma and persistence as she truly believes that hard work and good deeds pay off in this life, sooner or later.

So many blooming flowers
They seemed like colourful towers
Still in the soil, a tiny seed
Patiently waiting, it had a special need
Others tried to make it grow
But soon moved on to another tow
With your watering can
And a patient loving hand
You took the time to see
All the potential inside of me
As I continue to grow
I forever want you to know
I came to be
All because you watered me!!

Choose Divinity for Life

Rajkumari Saharia

"A healers power stems not from any special ability, but from maintaining the courage and awareness to embody and express the universal healing power that every human being naturally possesses"

Holistic health is based on the idea that true health comes from a balance of the body and mind and renowned facilitator **Rajkumari Saharia** truly believes in the same. An ace hypnotherapist (CHII), Past Life Regression Therapist (Life University), Aura Photographer, Redikall Healer, Soul Temple Healer, Numerologist, Sound Healer, Rebirthing and Tarot card reader, she has been practicing the above mentioned healing modalities since more than a decade.

According to her, we never really realize that there is a certain strong energy that flows through all of us and this energy or force is intimately connected to our well being and has the power to heal us without having to take any outside help. Rajkumari Saharia believes that she is just a bridge in between the healer and the person looking for healing. She senses this energy and force among people and guides them to use the same for their betterment.

As a Chairperson of FICCI Flo Kolkata and a Past President of Lions Club of Calcutta Greater, Rajkumari Saharia has had the chance to meet innumerable people in her life who have given her some inspiration and have made her believe strongly in the fact that we all have the ability to create our own universe. She believes that it's not intentional that successful people are successful. They have attained success because they created their own map of success with intentional thoughts and purposeful planning. Everyone experiences the desire to create. However, too often we feel as if we lack the ability to create anything at all. So we lose faith in our own creative nature and here is when people like Rajkumari Saharia act as catalysts to help us realize your potential.

From childhood, she learned various lessons on being compassionate, humane, trustworthy, on serving mankind and much more. Where she saw extremes of both worlds positive and negative, she feels herself to be lucky to have immense teachings in her lifetime which have transformed her into what she is today. Very rarely would you find children so inclined towards greater learnings, curious about the spiritual world and believing in things they can't see, but Rajkumari from a very early age had an incredible sense of wonder - like an innate social being. Her young and innocent mind brimming with curiosity, with an inclination to appreciate and be enthralled by life experiences, attracted her first master to her. Where disciples have been choosing their masters since era's, Rajkumari was actually the chosen one. Her masters saw pure qualities in her in their truest forms and the definitive features of spirituality. These formative years nurtured and encouraged the naïve Rajkumari to step into adulthood where she was again lucky to get masters who continuously taught her ways to be the best version of herself, along with serving people around her.

Marriage did not stop her from pursuing what pleased her the most, and she continued learning about the subtle beauty of life, something like watching the rays of the setting sun illuminate our skies in many hues. Motherhood and other responsibilities made her pause for a few years but she strongly believes that those years were brimming with life experiences which in turn were preparing her to connect with her inner self.

Even though she faced various difficulties in life and she always tried to prove herself in front of others, but soon she came to terms with the fact that she did not need to prove herself any longer. What she actually needed to do was to improve every step of the way. Don't we all have these stages in our lives when we obsess over what other people think of us? She feels that at some point or the other, we have to accept that if we are spending our life trying to prove ourselves to others, then it's probably our approval that we are lacking. Just the way she heard a little voice inside her saying that love is a conditional thing and proving yourself is more of a constantly shifting target, she urges everyone around her to have the same views because once you do that, you will gradually start walking on the path of success.

The world is full of people feeling mentally unstable due to stress, anxiety and fear and this is specially on the rise at present when people are going through such a terrible pandemic situation. At this time, people around need healing and for that they need to open up about their innermost fears and share stories without the feeling of being judged by the listener. Ms. Saharia is a patient and empathetic listener who helps people open up to their secrets which they have kept guarded for long.

Rajkumari Saharia wants to spread the message of how to be and remain human. We are so busy in chasing various things in life that the things which actually make us happy have taken a back seat. We wait our whole life for something magical to happen, waiting for our lives to begin and in the bargain we completely ignore the present. We forget to live in the moment and forget that this is where our happiness lies. This is where our peace can be found. And, because we cannot find the happiness and peace we are looking for, we tend to get anxious and stressed. She wants to create more facilitators and spread the knowledge, so as to bring peace and harmony in the world with a healthy body and mind. The fact is that people of this beautiful and magical planet need to start looking within themselves more, and outside themselves less. It is the heart that makes a man rich. He is rich according to what he is, not according to what he has. Rajkumari believes that by doing this, we will all go back to feeling alive, go back to feeling refreshed, renewed and rejuvenated and similarly the world around us will feel the same way too. Soon, the situation will be something like Heal Self, Heal All.

"You find peace not by rearranging the circumstances of your life, but by realizing who you are at the deepest level"

A person travels above, through infinite space,
In their space suit, looking for something.
They look left and right, forward and back,
And they are spotted by someone who's watching.

"What is it you need?" someone calls after them,
As they look up to notice the person,
"I'm going on a search to find infinite space!"
Comes the reply shouted down with assertion.

"Stop and look around, you are already there,"
Comes the call from the quiet spectator.
"Leave me alone, I'm so nearly there!"
He will find the infinite later.

He goes on his search, travels for years,
Visiting all of the galaxies,
Never realising that his sought-after infinite space
Is the very space that he travels in.

Woman with the midas touch

Chaitali Das

"You want to be the pebble in the pond that creates the ripple for change"

The secret to living is giving. Anyone contributing to the wellbeing of others, communities and the world at large is sure to find more meaning in life. Innumerable people from across the globe have chosen to share their expertise towards communities and causes that need support. In many countries all over the world, women are much more involved in businesses with a social impact than in traditional companies. A major difference that was found between male and female led social enterprises seemed to indicate that women were actually more innovative. This suggests that due to their specific sensitivity towards social needs, women social entrepreneurs are notable lead innovators.

One such example of a woman social entrepreneur blessed with the power to empower others is, **Chaitali Das** – the woman with a midas touch. Great granddaughter of an Hon'ble Judge and daughter of a public prosecutor and professor of law, Chaitali was surrounded by legal practitioners during her growing up years. As a child, she was lucky to have visited her father in the Alipore Police Court. This 'one time' visit could have been shrugged off by young Chaitali as something that held no importance for her, but a sight caught her attention that day and changed her outlook towards life forever. She noticed some people getting off a police van, handcuffed and with a thick rope tied around their waists. Chaitali just stood their dumbfounded as she saw the family members and loved ones of those prisoners trying to reach them but failing every time as the policemen were not allowing them to go anywhere near their family members. She noticed and understood the humiliation and trauma that had branded those under trials. The ordeal of their families and the stigma they would have to live with all through their lives, shook and disturbed her immensely and prompted her to initiate her thoughts on how to reform the prison inmates. Thus began a journey of not just helping to de-stigmatize the existence of jail inmates but also to rehabilitate and empower the less fortunate, along with advocating and promoting jute, as a fashionable eco-friendly alternative to non-biodegradables. Who knew that at such a tender age, Chaitali had set out to earn the epithet of 'Jute Revivalist'.

It is said that family plays a very important role when you set out to do something different. If the family is supportive, the most difficult journey feels like a cakewalk. Chaitali considers herself exceptionally lucky as her philanthropic and socially responsible zeal found a match in her husband, a businessman who supported her with funding and guided her throughout.

As the managing trustee of Rakshak Foundation, Chaitali has worked extensively in various humanitarian services, women empowerment and inclusive growth. From the beginning, she always aspired to do more, and in the year 2016, the government of West Bengal gave her foundation permission to work in the Alipore Womens Correctional Home to provide vocational training to the jail inmates. Working with prisoners was of course not easy and Chaitali had to face numerous hurdles on the way but she was not someone who could be stopped and she went ahead with her mission with a firm resolve. In the year 2017, she began working towards bringing an eco-friendly green revolution behind the massive barricades of confinement and thus her resolve to bring about a change, resulted in the launch of her dream project 'Jute Story Behind Bars' (JSBB).

Some of the obstacles she faced till here were quite hard hitting such as social isolation in her business circles, and disdained for working with convicts. She was discouraged for her decision to work on reviving jute and was told it was unworthy as it constituted a dying industry along with a very basic material to work with. These demoralizing viewpoints did not dissuade her at all and she quietly went on with her work. The challenges did not end here as the outside world was not the only thing that needed to be dealt with, as inside the jail premises the inmates were not very welcoming too. They were obviously used to a certain kind of lifestyle and to have someone intrude into their privacy, was not welcome at all. The project ended up facing huge wastage of raw material and time due to the reluctance from the prisoners. Gradually, she managed to break into the invisible tall walls that the inmates had built around them and Chaitali began training them through ongoing workshops under the aegis of her foundation.

Thinking out of the box has always been Chaitali's forte and she again managed to create a huge buzz in the City of Joy Kolkata, by introducing 'Paat Rani' the heritage tram. Literally meaning the Queen of Jute, this project was conceptualized as an innovative store-on-wheels, for showcasing diversified products crafted out of jute. Unlike her previous project, this one received immense appreciation and applause. According to Chaitali, Paat Rani is a larger than life mobile extravaganza of diversified jute products on board. This project aims at mixing an old mode of transportation with a handicraft cash crop. Prior to this, she had also promoted jute in the floating store at Patuli.

Chaitali has innumerable laurels to her credit too, such as being the holder of the extremely prestigious Guinness Book of World Records for the largest jute bag in the world. Along with this, she is the first ever fortune most powerful women, UN/State Department alumna from West Bengal. She has led the first ever All Women's delegation and a non-profit organization delegation in two consecutive years to China. She has advocated and promoted jute in various prestigious platforms in countries like US, Netherlands, Canada, Bulgaria, Czechoslovakia, Dubai, Sri Lanka to name a few.

As an outstanding woman of substance and making a quintessential mark as a revivalist and reformer, Chaitali has faced her own share of gender discrimination and alienation as she paved her way into the field of social entrepreneurship. But with fire in her soul and an unmatched ability to think out of the box, she not only persuaded her friends and family to understand her point of view and encourage her in all her endeavours but also amazingly grabbed the attention of the society including the naysayers and compelled them to applaud the good work being done by her. Once she had successfully established a mark for herself, she began to relentlessly make progress in her chosen path.

After having been in the field of social welfare since years and having showcased jute in fashion shows on prestigious national and international platforms to conceiving unique and innovative ideas on how to promote jute, advocate eco-conservation and reform the society, the down to earth and kind hearted Jute

Revivalist. Chaitali Das has a heart warming message for the society and for the younger generation. It's her passion to see Indian jute products reach across the globe and to see the eco-friendly tram, back with a bang on the roads of Kolkata. Chaitali wants to remind people that both jute and the tram are our resources, our heritage and the charm of the City of Joy, so the citizens of Kolkata, along with the younger generation need to work together towards the revival and reformation of our rich heritage.

Chaitali's kind hearted persona has not only mesmerized and inspired many people around her but the way she so humbly interacted with all those who came in contact with her, motivated innumerable people to emulate her. During Cyclone Amphan and the pandemic when people were confined to their homes, Chaitali extended a helping hand to all those who needed support. Chaitali Das is a woman who has made a real difference to the world and she is surely a role model for many upcoming social entrepreneurs.

This beautiful quote sums up Chaitali's successful social entrepreneurial journey in an extremely profound way – "When you truly believe in yourself and your potential, then any decision you make, will be the right one."

The road to success is paved with tests,
So you've got to believe in yourself above the rest.
Dream big, and let your passion shine,
If you don't, you won't end up with a dime.
Challenge the status quo, disrupt the market and say YES!
And remember that innovation is an endless quest.

Don't forget to change business for good,
If you want to change the world then you should.
If you think with your head and listen to your heart,
I promise you'll get off to a flying start.
Make bold moves, but always play fair,
Always say please and thank you – it's cool to care.
Do what you love and love what you do,
This advice is nothing new.
Now, stop worrying about whether your work will be a hit,
Rise to the challenge and say "let's just do it!'

She believed she could, so she did!!

Barnali Banerjee

"As we lose ourselves in the services of others, we discover our own lives and our own happiness"

The foundation of social work is laid on noble purposes and provides rewards that can sometimes seem short or insufficient in the face of challenging circumstances. Social workers are a part of the few who do care. They care about social injustices committed every day and they are the ones who care enough to believe they can make the world a better place. Such is the story of 56 year old **Barnali Banerjee**, who is a teacher by profession but a philanthropist by heart and soul.

Barnali did her schooling from Baranagar Rajkumari Memorial Girls' High School and completed her Higher Secondary in Pure Science from Vidyasagar College. She pursued an Honours course in Economics with Statistics and Mathematics from Jaipuria College and then went on to complete her Masters in Economics and Bachelors in Education (B.Ed) from Calcutta University.

It is said that 'charity begins at home' and this is exactly the value that was given to Barnali as a child. From sharing her clothes, books and toys with the less fortunate kids in her neighbourhood, little Barnali was taught by her parents to treat all fellow citizens as equals and to remember that whatever she possessed was to be shared with those who did not have access to some minor and major necessities in life. During the massive and devastating flood in the year 1978, 14 year old Barnali escorted her mom and dad to innumerable localities around her home to distribute items of necessity to families who had suffered immense destruction due to the floods. Barnali collaborates Belur Math on various social activities (i.e. organizing student workshops to inspire them along the humanitarian act of Sister Nivedita.)

Barnali has been an all-rounder since her very childhood, in addition to excelling her academics she aced her extra-curricular activities. She had a keen interest in sports, locally she is known as a sportsperson. Further she is a trained National Cadet Corps (NCC). She took classical songs training from Pandit Harihar Shukla. She also learnt to dance and recite from her mother who is also an artist. Barnali has performed at numerous events and she has organized 70+ stage shows more than often with people who never knew how to sing or dance ranging from various walks of life (3 years old to 72 years old).

Barnali can be called a born teacher as she loved imparting knowledge to her classmates during her college days and she would often leave her peers wondering about her capability to explain the most difficult numerical with utmost ease. Even though she was teaching needy children before her marriage, her formal teaching career began from St. Ninians High School for girls, where she was given the task of teaching mathematics and science to secondary students. Waving her magical wand, she succeeded in improving the overall results of her school. From here, she went on to become the principal of Shishu Vihar Primary School in Dum Dum. During her teaching career, she witnessed a harsh reality of parents putting unreasonable pressure on young children for good academic results. Having lived by the principles of overall growth through extra-curricular and social activities and sports, she started teaching the same to her students and counselling their guardians. This not only helped her students to find their paths in life who have now grown to become doctor, police, singer etc. but also made her a role model in their lives as they continue teaching the importance of overall growth to their children and younger ones. However, Barnali doesn't believe her work here is done as she continues to sensitize parents on the perils of undue academic pressure on their wards.

Being staunch followers of Swami Vivekananda and Netaji Subhash Chandra Bose, Barnali's father taught her to love unconditionally, reinforce the importance of giving back to the society, become a better version of oneself and to respect the country you live in. At the age of 30, Barnali felt an eternal change in her life when she came under the divine grace of Sree Sree Mohanananda Brahmachari Maharaj. His preaching of service above self and social work encouraged her to devote herself to help the needy. Sree Sree Mohanananda Maharaj had established hospitals to provide free treatment to the poor and Barnali is actively involved in the upgradation of some of these such as Balananda Hospital in Behala. Recently she arranged for additional oxygen concentrators in the hospital to ensure treatment of poor people amidst the oxygen shortage during the pandemic.

Sree Sree Mohananda Maharaj emphasized on the value of free and quality education of the underprivileged as the future of society is tied to the upbringing of our future generations. Inspired by this, Barnali left her full-time job as the principal of Sishu Bihar and started a primary school for the underprivileged children of her locality and named it after her guruji, "*Mohan Academy*". Barnali joined hands with Rotary Club to provide her students fresh set of bedding, pair of clothes and necessary stationary every year. It gives her immense pride that many students from this school are making a decent living today, for instance, one of the students has a coaching centre of his own while another is working at a poly clinic.

Barnali joined Rotary Club in 2011, so that she could amplify her social impact and outreach. Few of her tireless efforts include providing relief to victims of natural calamities (e.g., providing shelter kits to 150+ families during Amphan cyclone, installing drinking water filters to the tribal areas of Sundarbans), supporting the growth of children (e.g., sponsors education of a child every year, actively involved with the food requirements of 2 orphanages, supports schools for special kids), looking after well being of the needy (e.g., organizes free medical check-ups which is followed by free treatments such as cataract operation, child heart surgery) and creating social awareness for a sustainable environment through campaigns on discarding the use of plastic, planting trees etc. Her selfless work has often been recognized through several awards and honours she has received from Rotary such as Outstanding President, Outstanding Assistant Governor etc. and other organizations such as Sanghati Club Belghoria, Kankurgachi Vivekananda Vidyapeeth for boys etc.

Barnali carries out her professional and social activities while managing her household all by herself since her husband's occupation involves traveling out station almost all round the year. Her mother and daughter have been her strongest supporters and pillars of strength - her mother taught her to be what she is today and it gives her immense pride to see her daughter live by the same principles and dedication to humanitarian activities as her.

Barnali wants to send out a message that everyone is born to do something in this world and as an appreciation to all that we receive from society, we must play our part in it's betterment. She is sure that every action counts and that one needs to make small efforts towards doing good or nothing would ever change. Being a good person is all about doing small things such as how you treat others, how you selflessly serve and help people around you. So, if we need to work towards making this world a better place, we must understand that one person cannot change the world, but that one person can change the world of another and the positive ripple slowly changes the world.

Mix a little shake of laughter in the doings of the day
Scatter golden bits of sunshine as you plod along the way
Stop to cheer a fellow human that's a bit worse off than you
Help him climb the pesky ladder that you find so hard to do
Show by every daily motive, every thought and every deed
You are the one that folks can turn to when they find themselves in need
Just forget the rugged places
Make believe they are slick and smooth
When you spot the troubled faces
Pull a grin and try to soothe
Life's a game, a mighty short one

Play it gamely while you can
Let the score book show the record
That you measured up a man!!

Pursuing Dreams, Transforming Lives

Amit Sharma

"A star does not compete with other stars around it; it just shines"

There are two kinds of people in this world. Those who think and those who feel. Fortunately, there is a growing community of those who feel and think simultaneously and believe that in serving one another, we serve ourselves in all ways of humanity. In the realm of social entrepreneurship, India has uncountable citizens who have on their free will, ventured into the world of social entrepreneurship to bring a sizeable change that they wish to see in the world around them.

Among the innumerable social entrepreneurs India has produced till date, Kolkata's **Amit Sharma** is one innovative and passionate professional with a zeal for business, a social outlook and the will to contribute immensely to social progress. Social upliftment and business innovation are at the core of his character and he has taken many efforts to shape India's tryst with social enterprise. Born in Kolkata in the year 1973, into a family of religious and pious priests, Amit Sharma was brought up with strong humanitarian values and developed an inclination towards social cause from the very beginning. After graduating from Calcutta university and then pursuing MBA, Amit started his own business in the year 1996 by the name of Dynavision Corporation, a small computer peripherals and accessory supplier from the by-lanes of Burrabazaar, the hub of wholesale and retail in Kolkata, West Bengal. With a strong will power and passion to excel in life, Amit did not take very long to establish a strong foothold in the business world and soon came to be known as not only a successful entrepreneur but also a man with a kind heart and compassionate nature, who was looked upon to bring a positive change in the society.

From his early days, Amit had a strong inclination towards helping the underprivileged in the society and had immense faith in the 'givers gain philosophy'. This humble and grounded attitude with a vision to serve, has made him achieve a lot of great things till date. His belief that education is the basic birthright of every citizen, propelled him to begin his work with the Dadhich society in the field of education and women empowerment. He has always believed that education is the key to empowerment.

Alongside this, Amit also believes that education is not just a need but a tool to alleviate poverty. Once the youth of our country is educated, then one can get employed in various sectors and thus go ahead to fend for their families.

It's rightly said – "If you give a man a fish, you feed him for a day. If you teach a man to fish, you feed him for a lifetime."

With this thought in mind, Amit has promised to provide employment to one lakh people by the end of 2024. He is slowly and steadily marching towards his goal and has at present provided employment to 7000 youngsters.

He strongly believes that as youngsters start working, they learn to identify their skills and attributes and judge their strengths, which in turns builds their confidence and self esteem.

Apart from providing employment opportunities, Amit Sharma is credited for introducing digital know how among the people of Kolkata when no one really had much knowledge of the digital era and computerisation. He had a clear vision of digital India from the early years of his life and hence successfully launched the first ever website for the Dadhich foundation.

His company Dynavision Technologies (P) Limited was the first master tally partner and tally authorised service centre providing total turnkey solutions for tally and customisation. With over 3000 installations, over 200+ tally partners and more than 100 Chartered Accountants as business advisory practitioners, he managed to carve a niche for himself with his social connects and passion towards accomplishments and the vision to be a successful man.

From a very young age, Amit Sharma took up leadership responsibilities at many organisations such as Calcutta Chamber of Commerce, BNI Prudent Chapter, Vipra foundation, Rajasthan Brahman Sangha, Concern for Calcutta, Calcutta Citizen's Initiative, West Bengal Welfare Society, Friends of Tribal Society, Rajasthan Samaras Manch, Lions Club of Calcutta Elite etc , to name just a few. He has been actively involved as a mentor with the Savera project, which works towards the betterment and upliftment of the less fortunate children of our society. Amit is also involved as one of the most powerful mentors for Shri Gandhi Vidyalaya - a school for children living in slums. At a very young age, he also became the youngest elected trustee of public trusts such as the

Maharishi Dadhich Seva Trust and the Saptarishi Seva Trust.

Amit has a strong keenness and will power to empower and give back to the society he is living in. Under this initiative, he has undertaken various projects such as Sarva Shiksha Abhiyaan, in the Sunderban area of West Bengal, SUDA, MORD (a project with the Ministry of Rural Development), where till date he has successfully provided education to 7700+ students and helped them with placements in renowned organisations such as ITC, CCD, Big Bazaar, Barista etc.

Amit has also served as convener for the Compass IT Fair - the largest IT fair in Eastern India and has also served as the head of committee for anti piracy cell, membership drive and IT directory in Compass and successfully ran a program for students of the weaker sections under his dream project – iDream.

With innumerable awards and accolades under his belt and honours such as Shreshtha Samman Award 2015, Dadhich Ratna Samnan 2016, Hall of Fame award by BNI global in the year 2017, 2018 and 2019, Emerging Lion of the year in 2016-17 and many other, Amit is truly someone who is set to bring about a catalytic change and with a passion as strong as his, he will surely achieve all that he has set his mind on.

Amit Sharma is not only a successful businessman but is also an extremely passionate social entrepreneur who has the right attitude and the determination and grit to succeed. He has set huge goals for himself and his organisation and is committed to achieving them, despite all odds. With a personality that is assertive and determined, he is one man who is focused, committed and passionate and this is what makes him different from the rest.

Success is not merely becoming wealthy.
Success is not only working for remaining healthy.
Success is not going after fame and name.
Success is not living life for such mind game.

Success is not just taking career to the top.
Success is not staying in a bungalow at the hill top.
Success is working hard for your dreams you believe.
Success is perseverance and efforts till you achieve your deal.

Success is having consideration for everyone.
Success is a strong desire and to live to help each one.
Success is to follow the religion of humanity.
Success is to always remember all pervading divinity.

Success is to follow the principle, "Live and let others live."
Success is to accept others as diversity of nature; beautiful and alive.
Success is working for happiness of the world, a dedication.
Success is to love everyone unconditionally without any expectation.

Planting the seeds for tomorrow!!

Rakshshinda Jabeen

"There is no greater pillar of stability than a strong, free and educated woman"

Everyone wishes to see this world become a better place and strives to do their bit to change the world. Education is an essential part of a living being, whether it is a boy or a girl as it helps an individual to be smarter, to learn new things and to know about various facts around the globe. Women education in India is the need of the hour for the overall development of not only the female generation but also for the all round progress of the country. Even though we call ourselves open minded people who are living in a modernized society, still there are people who rarely want to send their daughters to school and once they grow up, they eventually want to see them married and settled. We know that the thought process around the country and the world is slowly changing and this positive change can be attributed to a few strong minded individuals who have spent their lives working towards the betterment of society by educating and imparting knowledge to as many children as possible.

One such personality is 65 year old **Rakhshinda Jabeen** who has devoted her life towards teaching girls so that they are not seen as liabilities or mere burdens who are supposed to be passed on. She has always believed that girls are the future mothers of any society and every girl who receives an education is more likely to make education a priority for her children. She strongly believes that education has a ripple effect of positive change in the community and the country.

Born in Jana, a village in Bihar on the 1st of December, 1956, Rakhshinda Jabeen, her grandfather's favourite grandchild was extremely lucky to have been brought up in a family that stressed upon the importance of education and supported her in whatever she wanted to learn. She did Intermediate from Tantibagan Girls High School, Class 12 and Graduation in Urdu Honours from Lady Brabourne College, Kolkata. After having graduated in Urdu Literature, she went on to pursue an M.A from Calcutta University in Urdu(Arts). She had a very busy life wherein she attended college in the morning, taught in school during afternoon and gave tuitions to needy students in the evening. She taught for a few years in an all girls school before getting married in the year 1977. She lost her father soon after her marriage and the responsibility of her siblings came on her shoulders. The emotional turmoil she went through during those days, also affected her married life.

Due to financial constraints, her husband supported her decision to join a school as a teacher. She joined Maulana Muhammad Ali High School for girls where she taught for 40 years. Soon she was blessed with her first child and gradually gave birth to two more boys but even though she was a devoted wife and mother, she did not let her passion to teach, whither down even for a second. During the years when her kids were small and she could not teach in school, she gave home tuitions to all her students who were missing her presence in school.

Besides her three sons who are now an MBA, Sound Engineer and MBBS respectively, Rakhshinda gets extremely emotional thinking about all the girls she has taught till date and who are now respectable individuals in their chosen fields. She has not let age bog her down as she is still teaching students in the comfort of her home. Students come to her regularly because they know that what Rakhshinda can teach, no one else can.

Rakhshinda Jabeen's motto in life has always been to serve all those around her, spread the message of love, unity, education and community service. She believes that everyone is born to do some work for humanity but many times we tend to get bogged down by responsibilities and because of changing priorities and due to our selfishness, we choose to bury our desires under the weight of our duties towards our loved ones. Rakhshinda Jabeen had dreamt of providing a positive environment and good education to her children, and she sacrificed her desires to help them achieve theirs. Moving ahead on the path of creating awareness about education and encouraging involvement in community service efforts, she co-founded Junaid Education Foundation (JEF) , a voluntary organization which aims to give a better tomorrow to the younger generation. JEF paves the way for school dropouts and helps them so that they don't feel dejected or left out. Rakhshinda believes that every child has the right to dream and those who can, should help them realize those dreams. According to her, the ultimate goal if life should not be to get a degree but attaining knowledge should be a thought that everyone needs to cultivate. Even at this age, Rakhshinda is truly a go getter who works tirelessly with villagers to set up awareness camps, provide reliable and regular health care for women and children.

Rakhshinda Jabeen is very passionate not only about education but also about life. She is very sure of one thing and that is 'she does not want to be dependent on anyone'. She could have decided to take it easy after a few major setbacks specially when she lost her husband and also during the time when she was diagnosed with a major illness, but she did not stop as she feels that her dream to create a world for children where education is free and without any religious bias, is yet to be fulfilled. She has lived a life of contentment and still looks forward to doing the same. It's a normal thought process that as we age, many of us start worrying about what living alone will be like. Questions such as "Who'll help me if I become ill?" "What if I feel lonely and isolated?" might worry us a lot but Rakshinda has chosen not to be affected by any of this and she wishes to be independent always. Not only for herself, she wants to give this message to all girls and women around her as she believes women have come a long way from helplessly sitting in towers, waiting to be rescued. She wants women to not be afraid of pursuing their passion and not to stress over being alone because if one plans accordingly and treads on an exciting path of education and independence, then the future is sure to beckon with exciting possibilities.

For some education is a privilege
For others it's a right
The difference between darkness
And a future that is bright

Some will think a burden
Where others see a gift
The key to moving forward
And to give your life a lift

If school is not your calling
Look beyond its doors
The world can be a teacher
Many adventures are in store

As long as you are learning
Your education grows
That will lead to contributions
As you share the things you know!!

Rebuilding lives for future

Saumya Varma & Mahima Varma

"Alone we can do so little, together we can do so much"

When you have such a strong legacy in front, you do tend to follow that path but only if your heart and mind think in the same direction too. And once you do, you are bound to get successful because you have all the right values and beliefs instilled deep within you.

This is the story of siblings **Saumya and Mahima Varma**, who from childhood learnt the importance of selfless service and decided to dedicate their lives to the same. They surely learnt the nuances of philanthropy even before they were born because they must have heard innumerable conversations between their grandma and mom where they would have discussed how to make this society a more beautiful place. Then when they took baby steps into this world, they came face to face with the legacy they had always felt and which was created by their Grandma, the great Kantha revivalist Shamlu Dudeja, followed by their mother, the very dynamic Mallika Varma.

This sibling works with their hearts on their sleeves and heads set firmly on their shoulders. They are on a mission to make the world a better place to live in and slowly and steadily they are successfully changing lives.

Let us first talk about the elder of the two, Saumya. For a 25 year old, she comes across as a strong, determined yet soft hearted woman who dares to speak what has not yet been said and has the courage to challenge the powerful and intimidating in order to serve humanity in the best possible way she can.

An alumnus of Loreto house, Saumya had always wanted to become a social justice and human rights activist. At the young age of 16, when she was in Class 10, she was a part of a project on universal declaration of human rights, where she learnt a lot more about the subject she was interested in.

After graduating from Haverford College in the year 2018, Saumya came back to Kolkata and joined Calcutta Foundation which was founded by her Grandma. Her philanthropy journey at the foundation began by working in the health care sector dedicated towards helping women and children. Under Saumya's leadership, Project Mayuri was initiated which worked towards providing health care at the doorsteps of villagers by setting up rural monthly outreach clinics across 4 villages which the foundation had adopted. Saumya, along with her team realised the importance of setting up regular health care camps, they planned visits by renowned doctors from Kolkata, made sure the villagers benefitted from follow up checkups and were supplied medicines regularly.

Once Covid struck in the beginning of 2020, Saumya realized the grave requirement for food. The daily wage workers suffered a major setback because their earnings stopped and thus they could not provide basic meals to their families as well. Calcutta Foundation began relief work by providing daily rations for around 6 to 8 months but they had to increase their work, when Cyclone Amphan hit. Along with Covid, Amphan created mass destruction all over Bengal, leaving people homeless, hungry and sick. The relief work that began somewhere in early 2020 is still continuing.

Under Saumya's able leadership, Calcutta Foundation has initiated 'Apni Kutir' which are basically community centres for women living in villages where they can learn skills, receive education and share their grievances with other women who understand. Besides this, the foundation is also providing short term employment in rural areas where villagers can earn upto Rs. 3600 by devoting just one hour everyday for 3 weeks in a month.

Following her Grandmom's, mother's and elder sister's footsteps is 22 year old Mahima Varma who is level headed, understanding and extremely humble. Like her sister, she also completed her schooling from Loreto House and then went on to pursue graduation from Duke University, North Carolina. In the year 2014, when Mahima was in Class 9, she like many other women and girls across India, suffered a massive jolt in the form of the Nirbhaya rape case. As a young girl, the case got her to think about the social injustice on women which was carrying on since decades. As an initiative of the Calcutta Foundation, Mahima began a self-defence and awareness program, 'Girls for tomorrow' to educate girls about their security rights. Even though it wasn't a very big initiative, it managed to awaken the society to quite an extent.

Mahima completed graduation in Sociology and Psychology with a specialization in Criminal Psych. In the 2nd year of college, she and a few of her classmates were sent on a project to Jordan and Uganda where they interacted with refugees and learnt about their life stories, as well as the atrocities they had suffered. The chance to interact with them made Mahima realize the importance of sharing stories. Once she was back home in Kolkata, she initiated project 'Apni Kahaani' under the Calcutta Foundation to encourage the less fortunate in the society to share their stories so that they could be helped. Mahima has also been working hand in hand with her elder sister Saumya on Covid and Cyclone Amphan related projects.

In March 2020, when the pandemic had just begun and Mahima had barely set foot in India after having studied abroad, she came face to face with the urgent needs of daily wage workers around the state of West Bengal. Project Mayuri which was initiated in 2019, now gave support to many communities through relief measures under-taken by the Calcutta Foundation. Very soon, she along with her sister Saumya, were able to send out kits with masks, dry rations, sanitizers, soaps and much more. In 6 months of relief work, she managed to provide relief to 21 different communities across Bengal to ensure some sort of stability in the lives of the less fortunate during the unprecedented times.

Saumya and Mahima Varma are staunch believers and followers of commitment, dedication, compassion and feminism, and together they have nurtured a dream of creating a generation of women entrepreneurs who are independent for life.

With each other for company, these two sisters are on a mission to create positive change in the society and do not wish to relax until they have fulfilled all that they have set out to do. In this era, where more and more youngsters run after the glittery world of corporates, Saumya and Mahima Varma show us a contrasting world where these young women have a vision to work for the betterment of the society.

They are philanthropists,
as simple as it's said,
considerate individuals,
with a passion that is colored red,

Charitable givers,
for those who are in need,
Positive entertainers,
with creative brains inside their heads,

There is no other word for it,
it is really what it says,
Cheerful philanthropists,
Living up such happy days,

To all those who aren't balanced,
they fix up the scales,
To all the propaganda,
they give truth to all the tales,

Though they are aware,
that with all the gifts they give,
they don't get much in return,
They will continue bringing back the peace,
simply hoping the human race may learn,

Giving is a gift,
of an angelic sort,
and to give this gift,
Is a caring thought,

So if you give more than you get,
but you give to those in need,
know that you are a philanthropist,
And you will help clear the world of greed.

The Earth Is Her Stage And The Sun Is Her Spotlight

Papia Adhikary

"Life is like a play, it's not the length, but the excellence of the acting that matters"

Theatre, drama, acting or jatra are all art forms that have been going around for centuries all across the globe. When the stage is set, actors are in character and the anxious crowds are waiting for the curtains to rise, there is a sense of excitement which is difficult to explain. Finally, the curtains roll up and it is time for the show to begin. Whether we talk about theatre, cinema or jatra, actors are a quintessential part of the same and have been enthralling audiences since decades. Generations and generations of people have enjoyed and appreciated good cinema.

When someone says Indian cinema, most people think about Bollywood. But while Bollywood is busy chasing box office collections, Bengali cinema dedicated itself to chasing cinematic excellence. From choosing unorthodox themes to portraying them sensibly , from picking complex characters over heroes to exploring new techniques of storytelling. Bengali cinema, theatre and jatra have set many benchmarks in the world and so have the actors.

An actor par excellence is Papia Adhikari - a beautiful and mesmerising Cine star and Jatra performer who has enthralled audiences for years. She holds innumerable stories of ages untold and brings forth various tales of life folk art even today. She was born in Kolkata and began her film career in the year 1985. She has always received immense love and appreciation from her fans all across Bengal. Whether she performed in theatrical plays, films or jatra, it took her no time to make a mark for herself. She played the roles of lead actor and supporting roles in a number of Bengali films and plays and left the audiences mesmerised by her fine portrayal of the characters assigned to her. Papiya has been the epitome of grace, charm and feminine authority on the Bengali screen and stage for very long and still continues to charm cine-goers or jatra enthusiasts.

She has worked in more than 100 films and television serials which included superhit one's such as Sonar Sangsar, Abhisar, Dipshikha, Protik, Protiboronguru, Pothe jete jete, Songashar, Drishti, Anay Abichar ,Prem Bandhan and many more. She was the only cinestar in her times to have acted in films made in various regional languages. She was also loved immensely for her role in Bhojpuri film, Ganga Hamar Mai and an English film, The Little Finger.

As a lead Cine Actress, Papiya was the queen of the 90's and was also fortunate to be brand ambassador for beauty soap Lux for 10 years.

As a theatre artist, she has performed in various shows which were superhits and ran for almost 1000 episodes, with two shows in a day, thereby creating history.

Born in a family where acting was a part of their household curriculum as Papia's mother was herself a renowned Bengali actor, the young Papia grew up watching her mother dress up for films and theatre and aspired to be the same. After completing her schooling from South Point School, she went on to pursue a Master's Degree in Comparative Literature from Jadavpur University. Even though she was a good student but she loved enacting and mimicking roles in front of the mirror, and this habit soon made her realise that acting was her forte and she dropped everything else to pursue the enigma of acting and theatre.

As she grew up and from childhood stepped into the shoes of a young and gorgeous lady, Papia was extremely lucky to have found everlasting love in her husband and soul mate Tamal Kanti Dey and unconditional affection from her daughters Suchetana and Sunanya . They have supported her through thick and thin and stood like a rock behind her when she juggled roles between family life, parenthood and her demanding profession. Papia was also lucky to not only have understanding parents but also very supportive parents in laws who helped her to maintain an equilibrium between reel and real life.

Papia fondly remembers the time when she had decided to take a break from acting to step into a world of love and marriage. Many directors failed to understand her decision, as married actresses during that time did not get meaty roles if they would decide to go the family way but Papiya knew what she was doing and decided to walk around the holy pyre with her beloved. She remembers how after her marriage, the directors and producers who would throng her place, started showing her the cold shoulders.

Papia chose family over acting and managed between the profession and personal lives equally. She was undeniably one of the most successful woman actors of Bengal. She played the lead in various movies, theatre plays and jatra's and etched an indelible mark as a powerful feminine persona and became a commanding presence in all that she tried her hands on. In the mist emblematic of roles, Papia would be an epitome of ethical superiority and portrayed a personality that had a class of its own.

Generally, the volume of films done by any actor underlines her or his versatility in different genres and their long love affair with the audience, but the sheer brilliance of Papia's acting, the range and depth of emotions which she expressed through her characters left the audience mesmerised and sometimes speechless. Many of her films and jatra's remain etched in the mind for weeks after one has seen them.

Papia's body of work in Bengali films, stage shows and jatra's are absolutely amazing. In films such as Sonar Sansar, Pratigna, Mouna Mukhar, Agaman, Pratik and many more, the ace performer has been proving time and again that she is unmatchable. Papiya has been redefining stardom in a way that few actors have done, combining understated sensuality, feminine charm and emotive force and a no- nonsense gravitas to carve out a persona that has never been matched, let alone surpassed in Bengali cinema theatre.

Papia has recently ventured into politics and is set to leave her mark there too. With a sensitive sensibility that no one can emulate, she's sure to do wonders in politics as well. She plans to not only shine on the silver screen and stage but also in the dominant stage of politics. Women need no success mantra and actually have an innate ability to master all roles given to them. Papia has been a star throughout life, so now her new role as a politician cannot be different. With many plans waiting to be implemented, she is strong willed and courageous and hopes to prove her mettle in her new role too. The world needs strong women like Papia Adhikari who can lift and build others, who will love and be loved, women who live bravely, both tender and fierce, women of indomitable spirit. She surely has the power to create, nurture and transform and does not only stand up for herself but stands up for all women around her.

Anyone believing,
A sustained career in the performing arts is easy,
Hasn't done it.
Or could if they tried.

There is quite a difference between being entertained,
And entertaining.
It's very similar to the art of writing.
And there is an 'art' to it.

There has to be a love connection.
An emotional commitment.
A joy that is heartfelt.
And a devotion that is inseparable.

If those factors aren't there,
Becoming a critic is less involving.
Less challenging.
And requires far less talent!
Being able to use one's body and mind,
Is a gift.
Especially if one has to tolerate
The creativity expressed coming from critic's lips.

A Queen in her own right!!

Malika Varma

"The heritage of the past is the seed that brings forth the harvest of the future"

Malika or Queen, lives up to her name. From being compassionate, hardworking, reliable, organized, determined, efficient and much more, she does as much good as she possibly can. She has taken every opportunity that came her way and has successfully paved the way for innumerable women who have connected with her down the decades, winning hearts at every step. Malika makes every cause her own – whether her mother's legacy or her own beginnings, she puts in her everything and grows with all she does.

In 2020, when the world came to a hold, Malika had never learnt to pause and with a determination that could move mountains, she successfully managed to provide employment and help the women artisans in rural Bengal whose lives could have come to a standstill because of COVID-19. Suddenly, Instagram and Facebook had to become lifeboats. Malika adapted while the world slowed down. She quickly gained control over the digital world, launched an Online Store to support the hundreds of women working under her and she initiated a the first ever lockdown sale of *Kantha* to get the wheels rolling. She spent days and nights talking to clients from around the world, building new relationships, spreading her roots and taking her work beyond all bounds.

Malika's forte lies in her grit and determination which she began showing signs off from childhood. With Alma Maters such as, Loreto House and College and

La Martiniere for Girls, she had the ideals of purity, of duty and truth instilled deep within her.

The younger child of her parents, well-loved and happy, Malika was always encouraged to have her say in the family. She was also lucky to have an elder brother who doted on her completely and kept all the best things in his life for her always.

Malika had always wanted to study abroad after School, but as they say God always has other plans. Her mother was diagnosed with breast cancer in 1986 and suddenly she saw her pillar of strength shaking, during her final year at School. God was kind and despite all the trauma the family went through, they stood strong together and sailed past the tough times. College in Calcutta was the only option. As things gradually began to settle, the family was hit with a new wave – another battle. Her brother, her best friend, began disintegrating as drugs started to take over his life. An unimaginable battle that took over their world, filling it with unparalleled fear, uncertainty, and pain. Every day was a struggle and every day they grappled to find their footing and keep moving forward.

Malika's strongest pillar of support in her life has always been her mother Ms. Shamlu Dudeja, the pioneer of *Kantha*. It was when the family was at its lowest, Shamlu and Malika together started the revival of Kantha over 3 decades ago and managed to make *Kantha* a source of livelihood for rural women in Bengal, under the banner of Malika's Kantha Collection (MKC). They put their lives into supporting this new family – girls from across the state, coming together for a common cause. Groups of rural women would huddle together outside their homes, gossiping or humming a Bengali song, and while doing so, their fingers would deftly create beautiful Kantha embroidery. Be it a saree, dupatta, kurta, stole or wall hanging; this form of embroidery narrates complex stories of folklore, legends and religious themes. Malika clearly remembers her first exposure to Kantha and till today the fineness of those stitches are etched in her memory. Thus began this beautiful journey.

MKC works on the *'dwar pe rozi'* model providing employment to artisans at their doorstep. With the help of team leaders in the villages, MKC has been able to reach the interiors of Bengal and provide financial empowerment to women there. The team leaders collect the materials, get the briefing on designs and go to the villages to assign work to the artisans who then work at a comfortable pace in their homes in between their daily chores and taking take care of their families.

Something that began as a community home craft, still works on a similar pattern with the only difference being that MKC started off generating income for a few women but today has nearly 1000 artisans who feel secure and empowered under its huge umbrella.

In 1992, Malika's family expanded when she married an extremely understanding man Sharad- a blessing in her life, who has stood beside her through thick and thin, helping her tide across life's highest highs and lowest lows. In a span of four years, Sharad and Malika lost seven people in their family including Malika's father, brother, and both in-laws. Amidst all this and in the tizzy of new motherhood of her two gorgeous girls Saumya and Mahima being born, and rebuilding her family, Malika took a sabbatical from her work in Kantha, giving up the reigns to her mother. Shamlu Ji rose like a phoenix from the ashes, as she went on to expand and globalize kantha talking it to different heights, making a name for herself both in India and abroad as a true revivalist. Thus she gave birth to her beloved NGO's SHE Foundation and Calcutta Foundation.

Malika dove into a new dream – another feather in her cap. In the memory of her mother-in-law, a Montessorian, she brought into Kolkata, the first Kangaroo Kids, an International Preschool. In a few months she was leading the foremost pre-school in the city with a team of the best teachers trained to work with children like never before. For 18 years, she spent time in the midst of children, who she says are the purest forms of joy, happiness and love. A journey unmatched.

Kangaroo Kids gave Malika a new identity. A platform for her to grow and conquer on all that she could lay her hands on, taking on roles in new organizations and making her mark in new fields. In 2018, she stepped back in with her mother to continue their organization SHE Kantha's growth to unmatched heights and strived to become a site for women's cultural expression through aesthetic means.

Unafraid to try new things and blessed with gift of the gab, she has charmed her way through life, one person at a time. Strengthened with an army of her people, Malika Varma's story is one of perseverance, dedication and compassion; a story that often goes unheard, a story that risks to be forgotten but it is a story of a woman who dares to dream and carve a niche for herself wherever she goes.

She rejoices in God with a grateful heart and a joyful spirit
She possesses the ability to genuinely say to another woman:
"I admire your qualities and attributes"
She is blessed with the gift of giving and a willingness to help others,
She consoles others even though she too is hurting!

She learns from her mistakes and acknowledges that she too is not perfect,
She speaks with words of wisdom and not malice,
From the mouths of destruction, her smile remains unshaken,
She lifts her head and continues to walk in the midst of turmoil.

She inspires other women to be the best they can be,
With her life experiences, she touches the lives of a multitude,
She remains determined to be the best person SHE can be,
She smiles every time she says "I LOVE YOU"

She has the courage to take the fall for another,
She is not too proud to say "I need you"
When her tears fall, she prays faithfully
When others turn their back on her, she still continues to pray faithfully

She is humble enough to admit when she is wrong
Through betrayal and talk, she remains secure in knowing who she is
She is loving enough to say "I forgive you"
She is at peace with herself without having the need to prove herself to anyone

She values her self-worth and reminds other women of theirs
She is not pretentious but instead she presents herself just as she is…
"A WOMAN OF STRENGTH!"

A Golden Gate To Success

Nafis Ahmed

"It's hard to beat a person who never gives up"

In today's volatile world, the only thing that is constant is cut throat competition. With the world population of 7.6 billion, all of them are competing to ace in the race of success. There are two kinds of people in this world - followers and leaders. Followers go along with the bandwagon but the leaders carve their own path, map their own road and embark on a journey of success.

Ideas might be the most commonly encountered of entities for the mind but entrepreneurship does not come as easy to all. A clear vision and an even clearer focus are the most important elements that can make successful entrepreneurs out of starry eyed dreamers. Fuelling their desires and translating them into reality is what some of the young entrepreneurs of India are doing at present. **Nafis Ahmed,** CEO of Golden Gate Group is one such name who has managed to cover niche for himself in the entrepreneurship scenario of West Bengal.

Born in Nawanagar, a tiny village in Uttar Pradesh, Nafis's parents shifted to Kolkata when he was four years old with the hope of a better living hood. He had a decent and happy childhood and acquired all his education from the city of joy. Having spent most of his childhood in the by-lanes of Topsia, he still cherishes the time he had spent with the people there, who were extremely supporting and cooperative. Even though Nafis's family was into the leather business, he always considered himself as an artist and saw himself as a sculptor who wanted to carve his own creations and landmarks in the city and thus began nurturing a dream of getting into real estate to start developing buildings. Therefore, after completing his studies in the year 2007, he ventured into real estate and started his own business.

Being an ardent follower and lover of numbers, he began his real estate journey on 07.07.07 and got married on 12.12.12 after falling in love with his lovely wife Amreena , an exceptionally charming and beautiful girl, who completed her Masters from Nottingham University in United Kingdom and who he says is always supportive to him and together they have two beautiful daughters Nafrina and Sabrina

Nafis has always been a movie buff and that's the reason he named his company Golden Gate which is derived from the Bollywood flick 'Love Aaj Kal'.

His initial days into the real estate business were difficult as he had no experience or background to support him. Challenges are everywhere and more so in the world of business where the risk level is much higher but if you have a will to fly, sky is the limit for you. This is just what happened to Nafis and he soared high in his business without the help or support of a godfather. With the firm belief that real estate being a creative business and full of opportunities, he began working on and developing projects that honed his artistic skills and at the same time helped him to accomplish his dreams.

Today when he looks back and remembers his struggling days, he feels happy and content to have achieved so much. He has a tattoo which says 'This too shall pass' because he believes that patience is the most important virtue in life and the toughest of hurdles can be crossed if you have perseverance and patience but always remember to have fun in the journey and don't take life too seriously as his other tattoo says "live the moment".

Being a real estate entrepreneur is not some magic potion one is born with. Truly, it is a means to make money but it is not a lazy man's way to wealth. Success can be achieved only through hard work, diligence, determination and calculated risk. Successful young entrepreneurs such as Nafis Ahmed who are doing exceptionally well in the housing market have an inherent ability to overcome obstacles and have a winning attitude that has elevated him into the creme de la creme of the society in a short span of time.

On a personal level, Nafis is extremely fond of super bikes and is a proud owner of a Hayabusa and Harley-Davidson. The Hayabusa was amongst the first few things that he bought with his hard earned money. Another hobby that keeps him engaged is love for collecting watches. His collection includes brands such as Rolex, Omega, Tag Huer, Tudor, Oris, Longines and at least fifty more. His passion for acquiring everything lavish does not end at just cars, bikes or watches, as he loves his aristocratic accessory collection which includes Mont Blanc pens, Gucci belts, Louis Vuitton wallets and lots more.

Nafis is a huge fan of Mr. Ratan Tata who he feels is one of the best businessman in India has ever produced. In his free time, he makes it a point to read Mr. Tata's books and listen to his speeches as these keep him motivated at all times. He strongly follows Mr. Ratan Tata's lesson that says - it does not matter what one does until it's what they believe is right for them and that it does not matter how other people quantify the situation one is in. One should always learn to figure out what their thoughts tell them and whether their set of beliefs will take them to the right destination.

As a message to upcoming entrepreneurs, Nafis wants to tell them to follow their passion and work hard towards their goal. As a young businessman himself, he feels that the best mindset an entrepreneur should exhibit is a well rounded one - one that has the ability to encompass every possible hallmark. He believes passing on the knowledge that he has acquired is the most important thing that one should do.

Nafis is extremely humble and a philanthropist at heart. He believes that it is necessary to give back to the society that has given him so much. With a strong belief in saying that the secret to living is giving, he contributes immensely to the wellbeing of others, the communities and the world at large. Nafis is one of the many people making a positive impact on the society. Even though he has earned big and is living a lavish life, he understands that wealth comes with a measure of responsibility to give back. At this young age of 37 he has been given so many recognitions including a Honorary Doctorate, Bengal Icon, pride of Kolkata, rising star in business, Young talent in Real Estate, Emerging face in West Bengal, Rashtriya Samaj Seva Ratan, The peace and social Harmony award, Real Estate icon of east, Bharat Gaurav award to name amongst many of them.

Nafis is an inspiration to many youngsters who wish to become entrepreneurs. By looking at him as an example, young men and women can learn how to follow their passion dedicatedly and diligently. Every upcoming entrepreneur needs a helpful nudge every once in a while so that they stay motivated.

Your work is going to fill a large part of your life, and the only way to be truly satisfied is to do what you believe is great work. And the only way to do great work is to love what you do.

Real successes are made,
Not dropped aside your door.
They aren't a thought you made one night,
While wishing upon a star.

Real successes are thought,
To be given to only the great.
They think that they work just as hard,
And they should have that fate.

Real successes are because,
Of someone making it so.
They fight for it and work real hard,
To make their successes grow.

Real successes are envied,
And rumored on how they were made.
People can be so jealous,
And even want to betray.

But you know how real successes,
Are built with hard work and care.
You've made your way to the top,
Everyone is so proud to see you are there.

Bringing fantasies to life

Pritam Dutta

"Some people look for a beautiful place. Others make a place beautiful"

A big occasion such as a wedding offers you a chance to share your happiness with others. You can't afford to lose these precious moments trying to co-ordinate everything the whole time. This is where wedding planners play a massive role in taking the responsibility on their shoulders. Their expertise and management capabilities allow you to cherish your special moments without worrying about anything. One such wedding planner is **Pritam Dutta**, founder Asparagus Events, who has created a niche for himself because of his resources, creativity, passion and enthusiasm to make your wishes come true.

Well known for his concept of 'budget weddings', Pritam takes care of the whole wedding from planning to organizing, and has a proven record of making every wedding, a dream come true.

While many vendors in the industry were planning lavish and expensive weddings, Pritam decided to take the opposite route. By identifying the most important parts of a wedding, he and his team focused on the concept of providing low budget weddings to those who did not have a big budget. Though the concept wasn't tested, Pritam decided to go head on into it.

Pritam grew up in Kolkata and his father is a retired government employee and mother a homemaker. After passing the class 12 examination from ICSE board, Pritam appeared for NCHM entrance exam and joined IHM (Institute of Hotel Management) in

Kolkata. After specializing in food and beverage and guest service management, he went on to pursue MBA through correspondence.

During the casual and industrial training that he had to undergo, he got a practical exposure to the hospitality industry. Event management being apart of the same, interested him to quite an extent and he decided to pursue the hospitality industry as a good career option. While he was still in college, Pritam had started providing trained manpower to a few established and well known companies. Along the same lines and during his final year in college, he would often take food delivery orders for up to 50 guests and this also gave him practical knowledge and expertise in the industry he was about to step into. His promotional activities gained him an entire wedding planning project where he was to handle an event for around 500 people. This was in the year 2010, and even though he was an amateur at that time, his clients trusted him to carry out the job well and he delivered all that he had promised, with utmost finesse. According to him, patience and consistency are the keys to his success.

Even though life has shown him various ups and downs, but he has still found innumerable ways to come out stronger. Comments like 'Bengal is not the best place for entrepreneurs' could have pulled him down but he decided to take this as a positive feedback and began promoting Bengali traditional cuisine on pan India basis and abroad as well.

Pritam has always been an introvert and although he is in an industry where conversation and communication are the main factors to take care of, he has never let his shyness get the better of him. He is forever thankful to some leading professors who trained him, guided and motivated him. He considers himself lucky to have acquired most of his attributes from them. His wedding planning company might be keeping him very busy, but he is continuing his learning process so that so that he can provide even better and more efficient services to his clients.

His and his company's USP lies in understanding the needs, aspirations and desires of their clients. They understand all individuals have their own thoughts and expressions but as a wedding planner and service provider, it should be their utmost duty to understand the clients demands and provide the best quality service along with a personal touch but at a budget suiting the clients pocket.

Pritam and his team believe in building and maintaining trustworthy relationships with all their clients. Pritam started the wedding planning services in the year 2010 and since then has grown by leaps and bounds in the wedding and hospitality industry.

Pritam founded Asparagus Hospitality in 2014 where they acquired banquet halls across Kolkata and provided end to end wedding planning solutions to people looking for something that would suit their budget. In the year 2018, he found it ALDP (Asparagus learning and development program) where they train candidates who have been have a keen interest in the hospitality industry. Once trained, these boys and girls are given part time or full time jobs in Asparagus itself. The Asparagus Entrepreneurship Scheme (AES), assists upcoming entrepreneurs interested to build a career in the hospitality industry, by providing them necessary guidance related to licencing, manpower, operations and sales.

Covid brought with it loads of hardships to people around the world but Pritam did not let the pandemic bog him down even for a second. He made it a point to keep in touch with all his clients by updating them with the latest lockdown rules and by providing them positivity in the unprecedented times.

Pritam plans to expand his catering services to Bangalore and Hyderabad in the future and also aspires to introduce 'Brand Bengal initiative' – a project to promote Bengali cuisine in India as well as abroad.

With such an immense passion in the wedding and hospitality industry, Pritam wants to tell upcoming entrepreneurs to be extremely passionate about the profession they wish to pursue. By gathering as much knowledge as they can, according to him it is important to learn about the pros and cons of each field before moving ahead.

A wedding becomes memorable because of a passionate professional who spends countless hours planning re-planning and understanding the in's and outs of the event. Wedding planners are dreamers and doers which is truly a powerful combination. By bridging reality with the dream world, they pull off some of the most memorable moments for countless people year after year and magically connect the dream world to the real world.

Dreaming dreams never helped,
Until we're wide awake.
To opportunities that flow our way,
Only for our sake.

Every moment is meant to be,
Spent in the finest mode.
Brick by brick we realise our dreams,
Through actions bad and good.

Step by step we move towards,
What we strive to be.
Our Future is a reflection of,
The thoughts of you and me.

Success comes in every step,
That we take to reach our aim.
Every step we take is new,
Two steps are never the same.

We get a chance to fulfil our dreams,
With every rising sun.
It's up to us, what we achieve,
When the day is done.

Time runs fast we know from past,
And is same for everyone.
Work and play, fulfill the dreams,
For Life is all but one.

A woman who decided to go for it!!

Preet Walia

"A woman is like a teabag – you never know how strong she is until she gets in hot water"

We all look up to strong independent women who not only empower and uplift themselves but also inspire the other women around them. Whether you are a working woman or a homemaker, life can be tough. Working women juggle between personal and professional lives and homemakers indulge in hard work of a different kind which requires a lot of time and energy. Homemaking is hard work and if you want a well kept home, you will have to devote time each day to caring for and cleaning your home. If you have a large family, small children, the work will be even more abundant. Homemaking is truly a beautiful ministry, a gift that you give to your family.

Apart from some challenges that homemakers face everyday, there are few women out there who actually cherish their amazing role and who have the ability to inspire others with there super women abilities.

A true example of such an inspirational woman is Banpreet Walia (better known as **Preet Walia**)who has been juggling between her professional commitments and personal life with utmost finesse. After having won the Iglam Mrs West Bengal 2020 – 21 title, she could have chosen to pursue the path meant for glamorous celebrities but she decided to prioritize her family and their needs along with fulfilling her passion too. She is also a finalist for Rubaru Mrs. India, where she would be soon representing her state West Bengal.

Born and bred in Kolkata, Preet comes across as a quintessential modern woman who has her head set firmly on her shoulders. When the Pandemic decided to strike our lives, most of us allowed it to bog us down and got engulfed by feelings of depression, loneliness, anxiety and many more but Preet refused to get herself emotionally pressurized. Even though most of the people around the globe were finding it difficult to cope up with increased household duties, Preet enjoyed serving and caring for her loved ones. From performing daily chores, she even managed to wriggle out time for mental peace in the form of spirituality. During a time when most people would unnecessarily scroll up and down on their smart phones, Preet decided to share her positive outlook towards life with others so that the psychology intake would not only benefit her but would bring some positivity in the lives of her friends and family too.

Covid was also a great chance for people to look within themselves and unravel their hidden persona. When some realized they had an amazing cook residing inside them or maybe a passionate singer or dancer, Preet was lucky to meet her spiritual personality and she wishes to pursue this as a future professional prospect.

Preet is extremely lucky to have found a wonderful and supportive family who has always been behind her, patting her back for all that she has achieved so far. It is said that every successful man has a woman behind him but Preet and her husband have proved that the saying stands true even in the case of a successful woman. Her husband has supported her immensely through thick and thin and has always motivated her to live her dreams and to achieve more.

It is all in the mind. If you can imagine it, you can achieve it. Time and again, successful people, women leaders and role models have emphasized the power of positive thinking. But, why only influential people around the world, even normal women have led lives which teach us that we can overcome just about everything by keeping our focus and passion going strong.

Preet is an amazing example of a phenomenal woman who wishes to work towards benefitting and uplifting as many women as she can. She is a true example of "We do not need magic to transform our world. We carry all the power we need inside ourselves already. We have the power to imagine better."

She works around the clock it seems
Washing clothes and cleaning things.
At times content, at times despairing,
But always there and always caring.
Taking on the daily tasks,
Responding to the voice that asks:
"Mom, have you…." you know the rest.
But do you know how mothers bless?
Women run a home, that's true.
But there's much more to what they do.
Beyond the making of a house
They make a life, they lift a spouse.
They raise up doctors, raise up teachers.
They become managers and preachers.
They raise architects, and builders,
Soldiers, presidents, center fielders.

Every daughter, every son;
The homemaker shaped every one.
Our lifetimes bear a female's seal,
Because women prove love is real!!

The lawyer who chose to make a difference

Md.Aammar Zaki

"To have striven, to have made the effort, to have been true to certain ideals – this alone is worth the struggle"

Most people have to struggle at something or some point in life. Some people are better at dealing with the struggles life throws at them, whereas there are some who tend to buckle under the pressures of life a little more intensely but there are few people who pave their way through the hardships to emerge victorious.

Md Aammar Zaki was born in a family of businessmen, pampered, talkative, naughty – just the way all kids are. From the time he was in primary school, Aammar would tell people that he wanted to become a lawyer. He chose something as different as being a lawyer and unlike other kids who are undecided about their future, Aammar was pretty sure about what he wanted to do. He had always strived to be different, different than everyone around and so as an excited primary school goer, he was under the impression that bring different was infact a privilege, but he had no idea about the inherent nepotism in the industry he was about to enter.

The only exposure he had to law during that time was courtesy films and television where he would look at the courtroom performances absolutely awestruck. He would love the lawyers arguing and talking to each other, the reason being that both were important traits of his nature.

Aammar's alma mater Frank Anthony Public School gave him a chance to excel in sports such as soccer, cricket, rugby, athletics etc, along with helping him hone his musical skills. When he reached Class 12, one day while having a discussion with his dad about their ancestral properties in Allahabad and Azamgarh, his dad suggested him to pursue a degree in law. A passion that Aammar had nurtured in his mind from childhood, came to him as the most perfect decision for his life and he decided to do some research on it. As luck would have it, The Telegraph newspaper published a 3 to 4 page article on pursuing law as a career for youngsters about to enter college. This was a major breakthrough in his life and he enrolled himself for a law degree from Surendranath Law College, Calcutta University.

When all the pieces of Aammar's life were falling into place, his family suffered a major financial turmoil to such an extent that Aammar had to act fast in order to pursue his studies. He took up a part time job with a US based company in order to support his family. He used to attend college in the morning, give law tuitions to young and aspiring law students during the day and work from 11pm to 9 in the morning. Even though, Aammar would have a tough time juggling between studies, job and his commitment to teach students, he managed it all because of his utmost dream of becoming a lawyer.

It's not very common to see people who had to struggle significantly, to become successful during their lifetime but these things do happen in real life too with those who believe in their dreams and work to make them happen. For them success is an ability to go from struggle to struggle without losing their enthusiasm.

When Aammar was in the third year of college, he left his part time job and joined a senior lawyers chamber for 3 years and being under his huge umbrella, gave Aammar an opportunity to learn the practicalities of law.

Aammar is not someone who could be made to sit in one place for long, so once he completed his law degree in the year 2009, he went to New Delhi to try his luck at the UPSC examination. He was lucky to clear the prelims but unfortunately could not crack the main exam. After a few months and joined a seniors chamber in Calcutta High Court.

His struggle was not yet over because he slowly began to realize the hardships that first generation lawyers have to face. With no real insights from home, as everyone in the family was into business, Aammar had no references and no godfather to help him. Aammar found himself in situations where he would think himself to be an ant at the bottom of a pyramid, waiting to climb a steep hill without any idea of how to. But he kept moving ahead with a strong determination to reach a position which others would only dream of.

If you are from a family with a law background, it is no doubt that you do get a well-established platform to practice. Not only is there the advantage of huge knowledge and resources at your disposal but there is also an added advantage of wide networking. On the other hand, for someone like Aammar who is a first generation lawyer, you are not likely to have that guidance, the relevant family ties or the connections in the legal field. Being in an unfamiliar terrain can be very intimidating which can lead to lack of confidence but Aammar is never someone to get bogged down under pressure and he slowly started proving his mettle to people around him and after handling a few high profile cases successfully, he took over many cases of serious criminal offense.

Aammar feels himself to be lucky to have been born in a family who has stood by him through thick and thin. His life partner, being from the same profession understands his passion and has always stood behind him like a rock, supporting him in all his endeavors.

For young and aspiring lawyers, Aammar is happy to share a few tips as well as some pros and cons of the profession. For him, the first and foremost advantage of being a lawyer is the financial advantage as lawyers are desirable candidates for varied fields such as academics, social work, commerce and industry etc. Along with this, the respect that a lawyer garners from the society is unmatched because the fact that this profession involves upholding justice in the society and standing up for what is right, makes the profession highly respectful. Along with the various advantages, there are a few disadvantages of being a lawyer too. According to Aammar, the onset of globalization and privatization has changed the profession to quite an extent and sadly lawyers do not have the monopoly in the profession anymore. The society is still to understand the importance of a lawyer and even though law tends to affect every individual in their daily activities, people remain far from reality and underestimate the power of a lawyer.

Aammar has recently founded an organization "Federation of Justice Defenders" to support lawyers and law students struggling in the profession and also to help the poor and the needy who cannot afford good lawyers to fight their legal battles.

After all the struggles and hardships in life that Md Aammar Zaki had to endure, he has still managed to achieve and maintain a great stature in the society and the beliefs that he followed all his life are worth sharing with all young and aspiring lawyers – believe in yourself and work hard. Keep improving yourself. There is no substitute for hardwork and dedication. Every field requires continuous improvements. Decide your priority, work in that direction and success will soon be yours. The only thing that one needs to remember is that opportunities don't happen, we have to create them.

People of spirit, people of will,
People of muscle, brain and power,
Fit to cope with anything,
These are wanted every hour.

Not the weak and whining drones,
Who all troubles magnify;
Not the watchword of "I can't,"
But the nobler one, "I'll try."

Do whate'er you have to do
With a true and earnest zeal;
Bend your sinews to the task,
"Put your shoulders to the wheel."

Though your duty may be hard,
Look not on it as an ill;
If it be an honest task,
Do it with an honest will.

In the workshop, on the farm,
At the desk, where'er you be,
From your future efforts, people
Comes a nation's destiny.

A Beautiful Marriage Of Art & Culture

Sanchita Bhattacharya & Tarun Bhattacharya

For decades, dance and music have held a place of primacy in Indian culture and in traditional aesthetics, these forms of expression are often allegorized as the food of the soul. Dance and music symbolise India's remarkable diversity in cultural, linguistic and regional terms and embody the historical tides that have shaped its contemporary pluralism. Music and dance are art forms that have permeated all aspects of cultural life in India where they play a significant role in the home, on the streets, at the temple, at social events and in festival celebrations. At a time when there is a huge demand for western dance forms, Indian classical forms are still going strong and this has been possible only because of the diamonds our country has produced in the form of music maestros and dance gurus who have kept the Indian classical art form flying high.

One of the most renowned, pioneering and revolutionary musician who has changed the face of Indian classical music is **Pandit Tarun Bhattacharya.** He is one of the most celebrated torchbearers of Indian classical music who regularly performs in concerts and musical festivals across the globe. Pt. Tarun is known to be the world's most prominent virtuosos of the Santoor. His father Robi Bhattacharya initiated him into classical music at a very young age. Even though Tarun's parents are both Sitar players, he first started playing the tabla and gradually shifted over to Santoor. When he was around eight years old, his father enrolled him for his first professional course under the tutelage of Pandit Dulal Roy in Calcutta. Pt. Tarun owes most of his technical know how to his father and guru. He was also extremely lucky to have trained under music maestro Pandit Ravi Shankar.

Well known for inventing 'Mankas' or fine tuners, Pt. Tarun developed various techniques to play the santoor that helped in it's quick tuning. This technique developed by him facilitated the playing of 'Krintans', 'Ekharatans' and 'Boltans' and also brought in the use of santoor in innumerable traditional art forms. Due to his improvisations on the shape and string arrangements of the instrument, people get to hear a more deeper and classical sound.

Recipient of various awards and honours, Pt. Tarun has the distinction of performing at innumerable national and international venues such as the Royal Albert Hall, Palace-de-beaux Brussels, Theatre De-la-Ville France, Apollo Theatre Spain and many more. Due to his continuous performances, he has a magnificent list of admirers which includes Prince Charles, George Harrison, Paolo Solaris, Amitabh Bachchan to name just a few.

Pt. Tarun found a perfect life partner in his wife **Guru Sanchita Bhattacharya** who not only understood his love for music and traditional art forms but also provided him the required criticism at the time it was needed the most.

Pt. Tarun Bhattacharya's beautiful wife Guru Sanchita is an internationally acclaimed and seasoned Odissi virtuoso who has been performing all around the globe since the past three decades. Her performances are well known for having the right balance of sensitivity, spirituality, classical finesse, lyrical grace and elegance. Her nimble footwork sad delicate presence on stage is truly an ethereal experience for all. Her kind and compassionate soul is reflected in all her performances and thus leave the audiences not only mesmerized but also craving for more.

Guru Sanchita has immensely contributed in propagating Odissi dance among the youngsters not only in India but also globally. She is the founder of Sanchita Dance Foundation, a cultural institute with a philanthropic edge that provides free of cost Odissi dance training to underprivileged girls and also takes care of all the expenses related to dance such as costume, music etc. Besides this, her foundation also trains young and talented dancers interested in Odissi dance by providing them a holistic perspective to the dance form.

Guru Sanchita has performed as a soloist at some marvelous venues across the globe such as Madison Square Garden New York, The Ford Amphitheater Hollywood, Esplanade Theatre in Singapore to name just a few. Among the popular Indian venues she has performed at are Khajuraho Festival, Jagannath Temple Puri, Maihar Festival and many more. The recipient of innumerable awards and accolades, Guru Sanchita regularly works with challenged children and works towards causes related to women's dignity and equality of status.

Pt. Tarun and Guru Sanchita met each other two decades ago and since then have stuck by each other through thick and thin. Pt. Tarun truly smitten by his wife's beauty is also in awe of her frank and forthright persona. As for Guru Sanchita, she believes that on a much deeper level, good music can only come out from a good soul and she strongly feels that Pt. Tarun's honesty, simplicity, humility and inmate wit are all reflected in his art.

When the mesmerising and beautiful worlds of music and dance collide, sparks are inevitable and the same happened when Pt. Tarun and Guru Sanchita decided to become two bodies and one soul. Even after years of being married, the beautiful couple are deep in love with each other where they share everything even to the extent of regular stuff such as a cup of tea or coffee. They call their relationship a fearless one where they can say anything to each other without fearing the others reaction. Till date, Guru Sanchita follows the ritual of touching her husband and guru Pt. Tarun's feet before stepping on stage for a performance. And As for Pt. Tarun, he looks forward to his wife's professional advice as the stature that he is in, people usually do not have the nerve to find faults in him or his music.

For ages, Indian culture has been immensely enriched with art and music and time to time this culture has gifted us with legends who have succeeded in touching the souls of many. Stalwarts such as Pt. Tarun and Guru Sanchita have been spreading the magic of their contemporary art for more than two decades and have mesmerised audiences with abundant shimmering sounds and ethereal performances. By enchanting people globally through their art forms, they have created history in the realm of Indian classical art.

Since the beginning of time, mankind has used music and dance to commune with the spirit of nature and the spirit of the universe and when these art forms are created with accord, their magic captivates both the heart and the mind.

Marriage is a commitment to life,
the best that two people can find and bring out in each other.
It offers opportunities for sharing and growth
that no other relationship can equal.
It is a physical and an emotional joining that is promised for a lifetime.

Within the circle of its love,
marriage encompasses all of life's most important relationships.
A wife and a husband are each other's best friend,
confidant, lover, teacher, listener, and critic.
And there may come times when one partner is heartbroken or ailing,
and the love of the other may resembles the tender caring of a parent or child.

Marriage deepens and enriches every facet of life.
Happiness is fuller, memories are fresher,
commitment is stronger, even anger is felt more strongly,
and passes away more quickly.

Marriage understands and forgives the mistakes life is unable to avoid.

It encourages and nurtures new life,
new experiences, new ways of expressing a love that is deeper than life.

When two people pledge their love and care for each other in marriage,
they create a spirit unique unto themselves which binds them closer
than any spoken or written words.
Marriage is a promise, a potential made in the hearts of two people
who love each other and takes a lifetime to fulfill.

Woman with a Vision

Neetu Bhura

Sometimes it is the people no one can imagine... who do the things no one can imagine

With the fast changing world, immense digital transformation has taken place with the new technologies and upgradation of new skills. At present, the world is full of work and the amount of workload that individuals have, differs completely from the past few years. Along with the various business options, a steadily growing tribe of women entrepreneurs in India have been marking their identity, across domains and industries. From conventional woman friendly enterprises like cottage industries to new age start-ups, women have started holding the reins everywhere.

India has seen a steep rise in women entrepreneurs but then achieving heights hasn't come easily for all women. From the neighbourhood auntie who runs a beauty parlour, to a teacher who conducts a tuition centre from home or a woman who is simply passionate about doing something different or has a set goal in mind, we have seen women do it all and much more.

One such woman who despite adversities or setbacks, dared to not just dream but dream big is **Neetu Bhura.** Born and brought up in Kolkata, she began her school life at St. Agnes School in Howrah, West Bengal, but later shifted to JD Birla. Soon after, her parents shifted to Chennai and she continued living her childhood under the love and guidance of not only her parents but her grandparents as well. Neetu's childhood was an extremely happy one where her grandparents doted on her and she was the apple of everyone's eyes. She spent the early years of her life in the midst of a huge giant family and where every little occasion would turn into a celebration because of the involvement of all family members.

Neetu had a creative side to her personality from childhood and drawing was a passion due to which she would often be found with a drawing book and a set of crayons in hand, wherever she went. She had always been attracted to art and colours and while she was in Chennai, she learnt the exquisite art of jewellery making. She perfected the art from designing to production and then went on to pursue a course in textile designing.

Neetu feels lucky to have received unconditional support and love from her parents Shri. Bijay Singh Baid and late Smt. Chandra Baid. They always stood behind her like rocks, through thick and thin and they were the reason behind her courage to try out new things and come up with exciting ideas for her future. Parental support is perhaps the biggest support that career-oriented women can get and Neetu was truly lucky to have got the same.

She got engaged to Abhay when she was just 22 years of age and marriage made her step into a family and household that had its own set of traditions and values. She was soon blessed with her two kids - Sneha and Vansh. As a part of a quintessential business family, her day would revolve around the needs and concerns of all family members.

The initial seven years of her married life kept her extremely busy with family responsibilities but somewhere within her, there was a creative block that saddened her. This was a block that regularly nudged her to enhance her creativity. Her family had also become slightly liberal by that time and the women of the house shifted from only wearing saris to now donning salwar kameez as well. The transformation proved to be a major turning point in her life as she began designing her own salwar suits with the sarees she had in her wardrobe. Family, friends and acquaintances started noticing and admiring her creations and began giving her orders to make the same for them too. Neetu did not know at that time that these small steps would actually lead to starting of her very own entrepreneurial venture. These small stints of creating salwar suits for people around, helped her launch Nvy's and slowly due to her dedication and hard work, the brand grew steadily from being homebound to shifting to a full-fledged wholesale factory. She then started focusing on retail work and supplied her creations to many popular stores, boutiques and also displayed them in exhibitions all over India.

Not only her parents, Neetu's mother in law was also a strong pillar of support for her. But, in the year 2013 her mother in law was detected with cancer and Neetu decided to spend all her time to take care of her emotionally and physically. Even though, Neetu was at the peak of her career at that time, she decided to sacrifice it all for her mother in law, because of her undying support and for loving her as a daughter. Although, Neetu was trying hard to cope up with the stressful situation, she received a massive blow when both her mother and mother in law passed away within a span of just seven months. That period was undoubtedly heart breaking but soon Neetu found respite in her new venture - Mystiquue.

Mystiquue is a hand poured soy candle and bath company. The setback Neetu suffered due to the two sudden demises in the family were extremely severe but the one quality that she thanks her father for, is strength. He has always taught her to face any situation with strength, grit and determination. Her father has been her pillar of support since she was born and has always taught her to be a hard working person and to never give up on life. These are traits that he has carried with himself always, which have helped him reach a position that he is in today. Her mother taught her to be a generous person and to make herself capable enough to do something for the society. Neetu wishes to be a replica of her father one day.

She is also a certified Sound therapist, Reiki master, Crystalogist, Angel card reader, Thamba practitioner and much more. She aspires to open a sound studio in the future where people can walk in to find solace, unwind and loosen themselves in order to lead a healthy and content life. Neetu has an endless zeal and passion to learn and create more. She loves to try out her hands and skills at new things and her mission is to grow Mystiquue to unmatchable heights so that she can provide employment opportunities for underprivileged people.

Imagination is the beginning of creation. You imagine what you desire, you will what you imagine and at last you create what you will. Neetu Bhura has always proved that creativity does not wait for the perfect moment. In fact, it fashions its own perfect moments out of ordinary ones.

A woman in business is like no other,
Multi-brilliant at work, and a great mother.
Guided by vision to make a difference in this world,
Reporting for service, with her hair even curled.
Ready to go, whenever the need
she knows in her heart, there's a calling to feed.
To do right, to speak up, determined to succeed,
A role model that plants the possibility seed.
Knows who she is, right down to the core,
Her essence, her passion—shine all the more!
She's in charge with a handle on it all,
At the office, at home, or at the mall.
Even in the depth of all she may know,
Realizes there's still plenty of room to grow.
So energetic, creative and fun,
Early to rise as there's much to be done!
She still finds time to laugh and to play,
Sacred time too, to kneel and to pray.
It comes from inside, driven by vision,
Get on board – she's on a great mission!
Her daily prayer resides in God's grace,
Serving others from her heart sets the pace.
Making use of her talent, wisdom and skill,
From strengths and trust in Divine will.
Gentle, compassionate, loving and strong,
In this sisterhood of success you want to belong.
Anything she puts her heart to she can do,
She's not alone sister – as you can too!
The road to get here has been quite a ride,
Call me 'Woman'– it's my source of pride!
Come along, she's blazing new trail,
A woman in business—whom we all hail.

Always delivering more than expected

Rajendra Khandelwal

The man who has confidence in himself gains the confidence of others

Life is filled with highs and lows, happiness and struggles that will test your resilience and integrity, push you to overcome challenges and leave you with lessons that will make you even stronger on your way up. It's the way you feel and think about yourself, including your expectations and beliefs about what is possible to you, greatly determines everything that happens to you. It all starts with your thoughts. When you change your thoughts, you transform the quality of your life.

Success does not come from what you do occasionally. It comes from what you do consistently. Always remember that if an opportunity does not knock on your door, then build a door. Because having such a perspective for life can help fuel new opportunities and business ideas. As many businessmen know first hand, great business ideas often begin as common pain points needing to be solved.

A successful entrepreneur strives to change society for good. Making money is an equally important dimension for them. Moreover, entrepreneurship if done right, leaves an everlasting legacy. One such example is of **Rajendra Khandelwal,** MD of Dhanwantary Medicare. Dhanwantary is a retail chain of medicine shops and is a household name for almost every resident of Kolkata, when it comes to healthcare.

Rajendra Khandelwal was born and brought up in Kolkata. After completing his schooling, he went on to pursue a BCom and MBA degree before going on to study to become a pharmacist. He started his career in healthcare with a job with the BM Birla group, who are the pioneers of healthcare. He joined their Calcutta Medical Research Institute in Kolkata, in the year 1973. His dedication towards his job made him achieve excellence as an administrative officer.

After working there for a decade, Rajendra resigned as he had a will to start his own entrepreneurship venture. From the very beginning, he was blessed to have friends who stood by him and supported him through thick and thin. With help from one of his dear friends, Rajendra managed to procure a place in Kolkata and opened his first pharmacy, Dhanwantary. This was in the year 1984 and since then he has opened innumerable stores across Kolkata and this renowned chain of retail pharmacy stores has served more than 3 crore satisfied customers across the city.

Rajendra strongly believes in the motto – "Serving customers with a smile". Mankind is his business, product is service and service should be done with a smile. He believes that service is the rent everyone pays for the space that we occupy on mother earth. Dhanwantary pharmacy works on the principle of devoted service with commitment and passion and this is what sets apart Dhanwantary retail outlet from the other ordinary pharmacies. He and his staff work towards meeting all the expectations of their customers, provide medicines of the best quality and serve with a smile. He understands that a customer comes to them when he is under stress, both physical and mental, therefore it is important to make sure that the customer is served with human touch and can trust Dhanwantary for providing medicines at a reasonable price in a nice and friendly environment.

Rajendra feels himself lucky to have a supportive and caring life partner in Shashi. They got married in 1984, which was the same year he had established his first Dhanwantary retail outlet. Even though he would keep extremely busy in his new entrepreneurial journey, she kept the home front going strong. They were soon blessed with two sons Rajat and Ravinder. Rajat is a qualified gastroenterologist attached with the Apollo hospitals and Ravinder is an MBA from Singapore. He is currently pursuing his interest in Ayurveda, herbals and pharmaceutical manufacturing.

Rajendra is very active socially and served as district governor for Rotary International district 3291 in the year 2010-11 and during his stint, he was awarded with citations for meritorious services innumerable times. Due to his dedicated services to Rotary, he was elected for the Council of Legislation to attend the Rotary Parliament in New Orlean, Chicago.

Even though Rajendra studied in Hindi medium education institutions all his life, he has managed to maintain a strong foothold over English. He never let this become a disability and instead he took it upon himself to learn the language, so that he could interact with the various friends he had globally. He's the Honorary Consulate of the Republic of Niger in Kolkata and has served as Secretary General for West Bengal Federations for United Nations Association (WEBFUNA). He has also handled various active campaigns for climate change, sound pollution and human rights.

Rajendra is a well known personality in industry and business chambers such as Federation of Indian Chambers of Commerce and Industry (FICCI), Confederation of Indian industry (CII), MCC Chamber of Commerce and industry and many more.

Rajendra is also a keen writer and has authored 'life is a celebration', an ebook enriched by the fascinating experiences of all the years in his life. Through all those, he gained deep insights and learned how to enjoy life. He feels that it was necessary to share those insights so that people would learn and be inspired to celebrate life the way he does.

Rajendra Khandelwal's story is one that can truly inspire young entrepreneurs to try, to start, lead and take tentative steps to grow and evolve their business. They need to take heart in the knowledge that no business is flawless, and the journey to success is long and winding. Most successful businessmen do take a lot of trial and error to get where they are today. Sometimes you just need a little reassurance and Rajendra Khandelwal's story does just that. He isn't an entrepreneur who sat around waiting for things to happen. He got up and made them because if you don't build your dream, someone else will hire you to help them build theirs.

Real successes are made,
Not dropped aside your door.
They aren't a thought you made one night,
While wishing upon a star.

Real successes are thought,
To be given to only the great.
They think that they work just as hard,
And they should have that fate.

Real successes are because,
Of someone making it so.
They fight for it and work real hard,
To make their successes grow.

Real successes are envied,
And rumoured on how they were made.
People can be so jealous,
And even want to betray.

But you know how real successes,
Are built with hard work and care.
You've made your way to the top,
Always be proud to see yourself there.

The best way to predict the future is to create it

JK Shah

"Your work is going to fill a large part of your life, and the only way to be truly satisfied is to do what you believe is great work. And the only way to do great work is to love what you do"

The nature of success requires ambition, a hardwork ethic, inspiration and motivation. Whether you are a professional or am entrepreneur, every stream has endless opportunities to make money, provided you have the capability to learn constantly. The only way to make money in business is not to be focused on the money itself, but rather, to focus on growing your capabilities as an entrepreneur. Success is not about making money, but it is about making the person who will, in turn, make the money.

One such entrepreneur who has worked tirelessly on making himself successful in all ways is **Jogesh Kumar Shah,** owner of famous JK Advertising of West Bengal.

After forming his company in the year 1975, Jogesh has never looked back and has taken each success and failure as a stepping stone to not only grow his business but also himself. Born and brought up in Kolkata, Jogesh belonged to a huge family comprising of his parents and 8 siblings. After completing his schooling from The Calcutta Anglo Gujarati School, he went on to pursue his B.Com degree from St. Xavier's College and thereafter, studied law from Calcutta University.

Because of a keen interest in the field of law and finance, he began helping his father in matters related to finance and also advised legalities and gave his expert inputs to his father's family friend, Shri. Ashok Sharma.

Mr. Sharma was the owner of Publicis Advertising agency and regular interactions with him, developed an interest in the field of advertising in young Jogesh too. Mr. Sharma asked Jogesh to help him out with his work and thus began ambitious Jogesh's stint with the advertising world. He began his company JK Advertising 46 years ago and has worked with all the big names and has rendered excellent advertising services to clients across West Bengal.

From the beginning Jogesh believed that advertising leads to regular enhancement of knowledge, your educational qualifications, your financial background and your family connections. Blessed with a dedicated son Nimesh and adorable daughter Julie, Jogesh has enjoyed a beautiful and fulfilling professional as well as personal life.

Business is known to be a great equaliser because it rewards the deserving and punishes the undeserving. Your efforts in business would amount to nothing if you are not a capable entrepreneur. Jogesh handled himself in a very mature manner in the very early stage of his journey as an entrepreneur. When young people tend to falter, Jogesh did not make the mistakes they would make, when they are unable to get desired results in their business and justify their own failures with blames and excuses. With utmost humility and modesty, Jogesh worked on his own capabilities and realised soon in life that money is nothing but your own shadow. The more you run after your shadow, the more your shadow moves away from you. The only way to get your shadow to follow you is to move forward. The same way, the only route to make money in business is to not be focused on the money itself, but rather to focus on growing your capabilities as a businessman. He believes that by doing so, you can add massive value to your customers and then, scale tremendous heights.

Jogesh's ability to learn has allowed him to observe, listen and identify the needs of his clients and business associates. This innate ability has kept him humble and grounded, and has also kept him stay connected to the requirements of the market and this habit has further helped him to stay relevant in the business. According to him, the key is to constantly reinvent and never get stuck in your comfort zone because as they say if you want to earn, you got to learn.

Jogesh believes that great entrepreneurs become great not just on the virtue of innovating a useful product or service, but on their ability to replicate their brilliance by building leaders in their business. Another ability that a successful entrepreneur needs to possess is the ability to inspire people to trust their services. These entrepreneurs have a conviction in their ability to make a difference. He has always lived by the value that a person's success depends strongly on his capability. The difference between what makes one business successful and another business in the same segment of failure is the ability of the entrepreneur behind the business. While struggling businessmen focus on how they can make more money, successful entrepreneurs understand that money is a by-product of who they are and, therefore, they focus on learning and improving their capabilities even in times of distress.

Jogesh feels and preaches that there is no small business, there is only a small business owner. Every business has endless opportunities to make money, provided the entrepreneur builds his/her capability by constantly learning, affecting their business model, offering relevant solutions to customers and teaching effectively to build a team and selling their solutions with conviction.

Jogesh Kumar Shah is an entrepreneur who started his journey with minimal capital, no external funding and no experience but he still managed to build a massively successful business despite all odds. Stories of personal perseverance, the ones where heroes overcome severe obstacles and achieve dizzying heights of success, have been around since the beginning of time but they never get old. Entrepreneurs such as Jogesh Kumar Shah inspire us and inflame our passions, making us believe we too can follow suit.

The road to success is paved with tests,
So you've got to believe in yourself above the rest.
Dream big, and let your passion shine,
If you don't, you won't end up with a dime.
Challenge the status quo, disrupt the market and say YES!
And remember that innovation is an endless quest.
Don't forget to change business for good,
If you want to change the world then you should.
If you think with your head and listen to your heart,
I promise you'll get off to a flying start.
Make bold moves, but always play fair,
Always say please and thank you – it's cool to care.

Do what you love and love what you do,
This advice is nothing new.
Now, stop worrying about whether your business will be a hit,
Rise to the challenge and say 'let's just do it!'

A Skilled Wordsmith

Sushmeli Dutta

"Poetry is the Spontaneous overflow of powerful feelings it takes its origin from emotion recollected in tranquillity"

We have all experienced certain emotions in our body that come together in an inexplicable manner and create a vision that is difficult to fathom. Since the advent of mankind, man has hoped to find an answer in meaningful words for this sensation. Whenever one feels this unrest, it signifies that you're either going to meet a loved one, or you are happy and afraid, all at the same time but quite naturally. This feeling of bliss that you want to put into words, but cannot, this joyful searching is in fact pure poetry.

Poetry is what is left to you after you have explored everything that you have within your heart or lacked a word for, or something that has made you sit down or pause in the middle of nowhere and has whispered the quintessence of the world and made you aware of your breath and your surrounding.

When you can feel all of the above, a poet is born and from within the poet come out words that tend to leave the listener or the reader completely mesmerised. When someone conceives poetry, that person does not remain the same.

There are many men and women who not only have the ability to write beautiful poetry but once they do pen down their thoughts and innermost feelings, they tend to become as happy as children because they learn to take joy from the simplest of things that surround them and they perceive the most wondrous of details. One such poetess is **Sushmeli Dutta,** who has been weaving dreams in the form of words since the past two decades.

Born and brought up in our of the mist affluent zamindar families if Kolkata, Sushmeli from a very young age lived a simple and content life. The only daughter of her parents and the only sister to 12 brothers, she was always protected from the outside world and this made her understand that maybe all girls her age were supposed to live the same way. This made her an introvert and she would stick around her group of close friends or family members. Her father Shri. Ajit Kumar Laha was a zamindar and mother Smt. Bharati Laha was a quintessential housewife. From childhood, Sushmeli was taught the values that every girl belonging to a respectable Bengali family needed to follow. After completing her schooling from St. Margaret's School in North Calcutta and College from Seth Soorajmal Jalan Girls College, Sushmeli was married at the young age of 19 to Subrata Dutta, son of another respectable family of Bengal. Subrata's father and Sushmeli's father were good friends and they had literally fixed their children's marriage when Sushmeli was barely nine years old. Girls during that time were not allowed to step out of the house a lot and therefore Sushmeli inculcated the habit of reading books when she would not be studying. This habit brought out another good habit from within her that was to pen down her thoughts in a diary. She would regularly sit down with it as she found it to be the best medium to express her innermost feelings.

Marriage seemed to her as the best option to gain freedom from the caged life she had lived all throughout but little did she know that she would be moving out from one Princess cage to another well known household that had its own values, traditions and boundaries. What kept her artistic side alive was her ongoing relationship with books, poems and her diary. She would often find respite in these and would end up spending hours indulging in her favourite pastime. It was only after the birth of her daughter Debashree that Sushmeli found the freedom she had searched for all her life.

Her daughter had an artist hiding within her and loved dancing and singing. To hone her talent, Sushmeli enrolled her into classes for the same, conducted by the Aurobindo ashram. This not only proved to be a great choice for Debashree but it also came as a massive turning point for Sushmeli. She joined the Aurobindo ashram library and got access to innumerable books that helped her to gain immense knowledge and also guided her towards becoming a poetess. She feels fortunate to have met miss Shantana Chowdhury there who introduced her to many people and also guided her in various aspects of life.

Sushmeli was an introvert girl since childhood but the Aurobindo ashram and her love for books, literature and poetry helped her to come out of her shell. She has written 11 books of poetry till date. Her first book was titled 'Swapner Rang Neel' and her latest release is named 'Mrito Jonakir Tip'. Besides writing poetry, she has written various short stories, features, dramas etc and these have found place in various little magazines such as 'Kritibas', 'Bhasanagar', 'Kabi Samellan' etc and some commercial magazines as well such as 'Desh', 'Anandabazar Patrika', 'Sananda', 'Unishkuri', 'Eisomoy', 'Bartaman', 'Pratidin',

'Nabakallol' etc. Her written audio drama book titled 'Srobon Sakir Katha' was published by Kalabhrit and many of her written dramas have also been aired on Akashbani Kolkata Kendra. Sushmeli also owns two audio drama organizations named 'Amader Uchharon' and 'Srabon Kathara' and is the sub-editor of Malini Patrika.

Sushmeli has various awards and accolades to her credit such as Utsab Samman in the year 2006, Kabi Nityananda Puroskar in 2017, Nigeria Smarak Samman and Dolly Middya Smrity Puroskar in 2018 and Kabita Singha Puraskar from Bangla Kabita Academy in the year 2019.

She is a member of Women's Writers Association since last 10 years which was formed by renowned writer Nabaneeta Dev Sen. She is also associated with NGOs such as Rotary Club of Calcutta Mid City, Inner Wheel Club of Calcutta Metropolitan East, Best Friendz Society and Aim Foundation.

Sushmeli Dutta is a poetess and writer par excellence and has enthralled and mesmerised audiences with her poetry and stories since years. She believes that training your mind is important so that you can see the good in everything. Positivity is a choice and the happiness of your life depends on the quality of your thoughts. Sushmeli is a beautiful example for women who wonder if they would ever be able to follow their passion but even though she started late, she never gave up on her talent and worked towards making herself successful in all ways.

You developed your goals and now have a plan
You know deep in your heart that you can
You may feel at times that you have failed
But by persevering you will fill your sail.

Continue to take it step by step
The goals you set are your prep
When progress is slow and you are feeling down
Keep moving forward and hold your ground.

When obstacles are around every turn
You must stay focused on what you yearn
You see success you will find
When you persevere and focus clear in your mind.

The mountain may seem overwhelming
Your dreams out of sight
But determination brings on a great might
Persevere and keep moving forward
Never doubt that the day will come
When all your efforts will be achieved and then some.

A life of humility, diligence and unerring compassion

HP Kanoria

"Vision without action is merely a drama. Action without vision is merely passing time. But vision and action together can change the world"

India's most generous citizens are no accidental philanthropists. The giving away of a part of your life and fortune is something that is carved within someone from the very beginning. Life is full of opportunities. There are opportunities to start something you, like a business or a family, as well as opportunities to make a difference. Many of the world's wealthiest people start their road to success with the single objective of creating and generating wealth. Obviously, without this drive and focus, it's very difficult to achieve those kind of goals. However, as time passes and the money continues to roll in, many individuals discover that there is much more to life than just making money.

This realisation can occur for several reasons. For some, it's a matter of finding a new cause or a new motivation. Others experienced life changing circumstances that send them down on a new path. Still for others, it is simply the realisation that they only need so much wealth to create and generate satisfy their needs while the rest is just surplus and can be used for a lot of good elsewhere.

One such individual is **Shri. Hari Prasad Kanoria,** a businessman and philanthropist par excellence. Born and brought up in an affluent family from Barhiya in Bihar, Hari Prasad had all the right values inculcated in him from the very beginning. First from his grandparents Shri. Hanumandas and Smt. Banarsi Devi and then from his parents Shri. Kedarnath and

Smt. Bhagirathi Devi, he received learning from all of them and thus began a journey which led him to the right direct destination.

He spent the initial and formative years of his life studying in Gurupathshala and then later went onto D D Maheshwari School in Burrabazar Calcutta to have primary schooling. He had completed Higher Education in a village Barhiya, Bihar. While he received academic qualification in school, he gained spiritual learnings from his grandparents. From a very early age, Hari Prasad was taught that spirituality was not about rituals and traditions. But it was all about the right way of living. As he grew up and closely observed his Grandfather and the way he conducted himself, one of the aspects of life that got deeply instilled into him was humility. Even though the Kanoria family was affluent and had immense wealth but they lived an absolutely simple life.

After passing out from school, he completed his graduation from Presidency College and St. Xavier's College, and then went on to pursue a Bachelor of Law degree from Calcutta University and became an advocate at the Calcutta High Court.

Hari Prasad began his business career by joining his family business in the year 1959-60.While he was studying and attending business, his father requested a close friend of his to persuade 20 year old Hari to get married. His grandmother and mother had also been trying to convince Hari to begin his marital life. Finally Hari got convinced and his family got a perfect match for him in the form of Champa Devi, who slowly and gradually became his strength, his inner voice and the wind beneath his wings.

With the unrelentless and unconditional love, support and blessings of his elders and his wife, Hari Prasad gained immense popularity for his humble nature and strong values. He's an industrialist, banker, journalist, educationist, philanthropist and social awakener with a mission and vision for enhancing spiritual value service to humanity and taking up the cause for women awakening.

Hari Prasad gets his inspiration from the teachings of Sri RamaKrishna, Swami Vivekananda, Paramhans Yoganandaji, Holy Scriptures and other famous personalities. The teaching of Paramhansa Sri Ramkrishna has always echoed "Giber Seva Ishwarer Puja" (Service to humanity in worshiping God) In spite of all his successes in life, he remains a true humanitarian due to his humble and grounded nature. His priority is welfare and this has always been the foundation for everything that he has ever done in life.

Due to his innate ability to turn everything he touched into gold. He's the editor in chief of 'Business economics' - a premier global fortnightly comprehensive and inclusive magazine which is published to highlight national and international issues.

Hari Prasad has been working on the theme of humanity, power and spirituality and has written two books, one book named 'Enlightenment' which was launched at the 4th World Confluence of Humanity, Power and Spirituality by late Dr. APJ Abdul Kalam. The second book named "All in One, One in All"- Religion of Humanism was launched by Shri Tathagata Roy.

He is the Chairman of Acid Survivors &Women Welfare Foundation India (ASWWF) which is the leading not for profit organization working for the prevention of all forms of violence against women in India since 2010.

He is the Founder Chairman of Shrihari Global IISD Foundation (SHGIISD) which inspires and promotes education especially among the weaker section of the society. He has founded Shri Hari World Schools for providing high standard affordable education with mission of plan to have a chain of schools. As managing trustee of Srei Foundation an organization in a Special Consultative Status with the Economic and Social Council (ECOSOC) of the United Nation, has undertaken several social projects in different areas supporting the free education of students, medical aid, marriages etc. He is also the Chairman and Founder of the World Confluence of Humanity, Power and Spirituality - a worldwide mission to serve humanity and inculcate human values and acknowledging the contribution of great men by initiating the Srei Samman awards.

Hari Prasad has been a member of several national level business delegations to UK, China, USA, Vietnam and Bangladesh, Austria, Australia. And has worked closely with various Chambers of Commerce and associations as president and committee member. He is the former President, Calcutta Chamber of Commerce and presently a senior committee member of Bharat Chamber of Commerce.

At the state level, Hari Prasad has received innumerable awards such as Sewa Ratna Samman Award from Dakshin Kalikatta O Sanskriti Parishad, Calcutta, awarded as a token of reverence of invaluable contribution to the society by Anandalok Group of Hospitals Kolkata and many more. At the national level he was awarded the degree of Doctor of Literature by the All India Shah Behram Baug society and Zoroastrian College in recognition of his contribution towards humanity, Millennium award from Dadabhai Naoroji International Society, to name just a few. Just like the state and country levels, he has also created a name for himself at the global level. He was conferred the title of 'Father' an award from St. James School London for his contribution to promote Sanskrit internationally, Certificate of United States Congressional recognition for his outstanding contribution to the society in the year 2015 and the Global Man of the Year in the 3rd Global Officials of Dignity (GOD) Awards at the United Nations, New York.

The value of giving was instilled in Hari Prasad from childhood and it has only grown since the past many decades. While India may find a few more entrepreneurs to emulate his feats in business, Hari Prasad's philanthropic endeavour's are unique and truly special. In redefining philanthropy by putting his money where his heart is, Hari Prasad Kanoria has shown the way for many businessmen not just in India but across the world also to tread on a journey of Enlightenment through service.

He is a philanthropist,
as simple as it's said,
a considerate individual,
with a passion that is coloured red,

A charitable giver,
for those who are in need,
a positive entertainer,
and a creative brain inside his head,

There is no other word for it,
it is really what it says,
A cheerful philanthropist,
Living up his endless days,

To all those who aren't balanced,
he fixes up the scales,
To all the propaganda,
he gives truth to all the tales,

Though he is aware,
that with all the gifts he gives,
he doesn't get much in return,
He will continue bringing back the peace,
simply hoping the human race may learn,

Giving is a gift,
of an angelic sort,
and to give this gift,
Is a caring thought,

So if you give more than you get,
but you give to those in need,
know that you are a philanthropist,
And you will help clear the world of greed!!

www.ingramcontent.com/pod-product-compliance
Ingram Content Group UK Ltd.
Pitfield, Milton Keynes, MK11 3LW, UK
UKHW041956190726
13854UKWH00005B/2015

9 789354 729638